The Middle Years of Marriage

LIFESPAN
COMMUNICATION
Children, Families, and Aging

Thomas J. Socha
GENERAL EDITOR

Vol. 13

The Lifespan Communication series
is part of the Peter Lang Media and Communication list.
Every volume is peer reviewed and meets
the highest quality standards for content and production.

PETER LANG
New York • Bern • Frankfurt • Berlin
Brussels • Vienna • Oxford • Warsaw

Vince Waldron

The Middle Years of Marriage

Challenge, Change, and Growth

PETER LANG
New York • Bern • Frankfurt • Berlin
Brussels • Vienna • Oxford • Warsaw

Library of Congress Cataloging-in-Publication Data
Names: Waldron. Vincent R., author.
Title: The middle years of marriage: challenge, change, and growth / Vince Waldron.
Description: New York: Peter Lang, 2017.
Series: Lifespan communication: children, families, and aging; Vol. 13
ISSN 2166-6466 (print) | ISSN 2166-6474 (online)
Includes bibliographical references and index.
Identifiers: LCCN 2017004263 | ISBN 978-1-4331-3344-2 (hardcover: alk. paper)
ISBN 978-1-4331-3343-5 (paperback: alk. paper) | ISBN 978-1-4331-4213-0 (ebook pdf)
ISBN 978-1-4331-4214-7 (epub) | ISBN 978-1-4331-4215-4 (mobi)
Subjects: LCSH: Marriage—United States.
Married people—United States—Psychology.
Middle-aged persons—United States—Psychology.
Interpersonal communication—United States.
Intergenerational communication—United States.
Classification: LCC HQ1059.5.U5 W248 2017 | DDC 306.872084/6—dc23
LC record available at https://lccn.loc.gov/2017004263
DOI: 10.3726/b11282

Bibliographic information published by **Die Deutsche Nationalbibliothek.**
Die Deutsche Nationalbibliothek lists this publication in the "Deutsche
Nationalbibliografie"; detailed bibliographic data are available
on the Internet at http://dnb.d-nb.de/.

The paper in this book meets the guidelines for permanence and durability
of the Committee on Production Guidelines for Book Longevity
of the Council of Library Resources.

∞

For Alex

CONTENTS

ACKNOWLEDGMENTS

Students played a large role in the research reported in this book. Literally hundreds of students in COM 417 (*Communication and Aging*) completed interviews and reports that are quoted in the pages that follow. They generously gave me permission to use these contributions.

A small group of very bright graduate students helped with an initial analysis of the stressors reported in Chapter 3. They are Amy Przytula Vynalek, Catalina Cayetano, Dayna N. Kloeber, Amanda Tuholsky, and Qun Lu. That work was also featured in a paper delivered at the annual convention of the National Communication Association in 2014. Daniel Kelley, an M.A student at the time helped by organizing the data, searching the interviews for key terms, and locating relevant literature. Students Emily Abellon and Chloe Kartes helped with data archiving tasks.

Cori Hart, an undergraduate honors student working under my direction, interviewed 7 long-term same-sex couples as part of her undergraduate honors project. Her research proved to be very useful because the main corpus of interviews included only a handful of same-sex relationships.

I am also grateful to Gary A. Beck, the author of Chapter 7, for helping me think more deeply and theoretically about these data. Gary's chapter contributes a communicative model of relational resilience that will help scholars generate new research studies.

I deeply appreciate series editor Tom Socha for his support of my work and for his efforts to create an outlet for communication scholars who study lifespan issues. Few of us can claim to have had the personal and professional impact of this generous and productive man.

Finally, my thinking about relational resilience was deepened by many rich conversations with Alex Zautra, a prolific resilience researcher, and in the last years of his life, a dear friend. Alex died while this book was in the late stages of preparation. I miss him deeply but am grateful to have known him well.

PREFACE

Alex Zautra*

In recent years I have worked with Eva Zautra to translate the research find-ings of clinical psychology to help people form meaningful and satisfying rela-tionships. This work is grounded in a long research program on the nature of human resilience (e.g. Zautra, 2009; Zautra, Hall, & Murray, 2010) and Eva's more recent efforts to update the concept of social intelligence, mak-ing it accessible to the general public in the form of an online public health intervention (Zautra, Zautra, Gallardo, & Velasco, 2015). Vince Waldron's new book, *The Middle Years of Marriage*, dovetails nicely with our own work. It confirms some of our findings about, for example, the malleability of social behavior. As our own work suggests, Waldron and his students have confirmed that aging dogs really can learn new tricks, even if that dog has been scarred by encounters with the sharp elbows of a challenging midlife. The book also expands our own thinking on how neuropsychological plasticity finds its expression in changed patterns of relational communication. Waldron details the kinds of communication that help couples resist, cope with, and thrive in spite of, adversity.

---

*Alex Zautra died before completing this preface. These passages were constructed from notes taken during conversations with the author.

Ultimately, *The Middle Years of Marriage* is a book about resilience, *relational* resilience. It doesn't presume that all committed relationships *should* persist though the changes and (for some of us) stressors of midlife. But it does wonder why some relationships do persist, and even thrive. To find the answers, Waldron had his students interview hundreds of midlife couples over several years. He reflects on this rather ambitious project in Chapter 2 and describes the resulting archive of interview reports and recordings. In Chapter 8 he provides methodological details, including the semi-structured interview protocol that allowed his relatively inexperienced students to conduct interviews that were both systematic and conducive to conversation, some of which became quite intimate. Students interviewed their parents, grandparents, aunts and uncles, co-workers, family friends and in-laws. The interviews proved meaningful to many of the students, some of whom had never experienced a deep conversation, even with their parents, about how marriages really work (or don't). In some cases the interview itself became a resilience-enhancing experience. It appeared that some couples were fortified by the interview experience, as if putting their relationship to words affirmed their bonds and readied them for future challenges.

Although he doesn't articulate them in quite these terms, Waldron's *The Middle Years of Marriage*, yields several themes that have emerged in our conversations as we developed our own intervention.

People are Hurting

As Chapter 3 reveals, nearly all couples, even those who would describe themselves as very satisfied with life and marriage, have been rocked by midlife adversity. These hurts range from infidelity to illness, from financial ruin to "failure to launch" adult offspring. The very ordinariness of adversity is in itself notable. Our own work has been motivated in part to address what we see as the widespread hurting we see around us. The reality is that many Americans are lonely. Many are looking for ways to connect with the people around them. And many need help in repairing broken relationships.

People Can Change

At the heart of *The Middle Years of Marriage* are chapters on how some couples manage to cope (Chapter 5) and grow (Chapter 6) at midlife. In both chapters Waldron describes concrete practices, both individual and collective, that facilitate this kind of resilience. Often in their 50s and 60s, some of these partners have bonded for decades. They are bound together by long-held roles, habits, and scripts. Yet change they must and change they do. We see evidence of this change in our own work. Provided with sufficient training, people can make adjustments in the way they value their relationships with others. Even at a late age they can try out new patterns of behavior and form deeper bonds.

Resilience is Social

No doubt, some people are predisposed to be resilient due to their biological make-up, genetics, or early developmental experiences. Yet, as Waldron shows us in Chapter 4, partners often work together to build resilience into their relationships, to ready themselves for hard times, and protect their union against the pressures that pull so many couples apart. As we see in the later chapters, in many cases this means building *new* social bonds, including connections to new friends, communities, and sources of professional help. For others, strength comes from *renewing* bonds that have withered. Reconnecting with siblings. Asking adult offspring for support. Rekindling neglected friendships. From these social connections couples draw support, wisdom, confidence, and strength. This book highlights the role of human communication in making these things happen.

As Vince and I talked about this project, it became evident that he is optimistic about the capacity of people to reinvent themselves and their relationships. This book provides convincing evidence that reinvention happens more than we might expect, especially when we look across the lifespan. I have been lucky to live long enough to experience that kind of change. I have repaired my share of relationships and, in recent years, formed a very special one. The relationship stories reported in *The Middle Years of Marriage* are different from mine and yours. In fact, each one is unique. Not all end well. But as you read across the book you will see that they are connected by the very hopeful thread that we call human resilience.

References

Zautra, A. J. (2009). Resilience: One part recovery, two parts sustainability. *Journal of Personality, 77*(6), 1935–1943.

Zautra, A. J., Hall, J. S., & Murray, K. E. (2010). Resilience: A new definition of health for people and communities. In J. Reich, A. Zautra, & J. Hall (Eds.), *Handbook of adult resilience* (pp. 3–29). New York, NY: Guilford.

Zautra, E., Zautra, A., Gallardo, C. E., & Velasco, L. (2015). Can we learn to treat one another better? A test of a social intelligence curriculum. *PLoS One, 10*, 1–17.

SECTION I

FOUNDATIONS

· 1 ·

WHAT DO WE KNOW ABOUT MIDLIFE MARRIAGE?

This first chapter lays the groundwork for the rest of this book by introducing the people featured in later chapters—those who are both middle-aged and several decades into a marriage or committed relationship. Chapter 2 describes the multi-year research project that I conducted, with the help of many student interviewers, to better understand how these marriages fare in the face of the changes, challenges, and opportunities of midlife. Chapter 3 identifies in their own words the kinds of adversity that midlife couples overcome. Chapters 4–6 focus on relational practices and metaphors. How do couples describe their efforts to protect the marriage from the challenges of midlife (Chapter 4), cope with adversity (Chapter 5), and grow from it (Chapter 6)? Chapter 7 (contributed by Gary Beck) integrates these findings with a new conceptual model and presents ideas for new research projects on relational resilience, the connecting thread of this book. Finally, Chapter 8 offers details about the methods and measures we used to study these resilient midlife couples.

What Is it like to be Middle Aged and Married in America?

Middle age, the period from roughly 40 to 65 years of age, can be a time of stability, but it is also punctuated by significant changes, and for some, serious challenges. Some of these reflect normative lifecourse events, such as the identity changes that may accompany the end of active parenting. Others are biological changes that tend to announce themselves at midlife, such as hypertension, diabetes, or altered sexual response. Midlife couples may find themselves vulnerable to economic forces and cultural change. For example, rapid changes in technology may necessitate a return to school at midlife; corporate downsizing efforts may disproportionately affect midlife workers who have obtained middle management positions. Middle-aged workers find themselves adapting rapidly to changing technologies and new ways of working, not to mention a new generation of .younger employees. During this period it may become apparent that retirement savings are inadequate, adult offspring are struggling, and a long marriage is becoming stale. And of course, those adult offspring may "boomerang" home, creating a new dynamic that can strain or strengthen a family and a marriage.

So who are these middle-aged couples? Well some are the parents of my students. And, yet, as I have learned over the years, many of my students don't know these middle-aged people all that well. For the most part they know mom and dad as *parents*, but are much less familiar with them as workers, friends, or the roles featured in this book—romantic partners. Understandably focused on the passage to young adulthood, my students don't reflect much about the rewards and difficulties of their parents' midlife. Looking beyond the immediate family, they may have limited opportunities to interact with middle-aged people. But students are not unique in their relative isolation. It turns out that few of us have meaningful encounters with people who are much older or younger. Although long-standing, this trend has accelerated in recent years, in part due to the role of communication technology in further stratifying the population by age (Strom & Strom, 2015). Social media make it possible for younger (and older) persons to communicate more intensely and exclusively with same-aged peers.

Lacking direct contact, older and younger persons may form impressions based on media-fed stereotypes of baby boomers (or Xers, or millennials). These stereotypes matter. As established in a series of studies conducted across cultures, younger and older persons tend to avoid conversations when their stereotypes suggest that such contact would be unpleasant or constraining (for example, see McCann, Dailey, Giles, & Ota, 2005; Giles, Hajek, Stoitsova, & Choi, 2010). The data suggest, as just one example, that the common perception of young people that elders expect deference spurs them to be polite but also avoidant. This avoidant tendency exhibits a "stair stepping" effect, increasing from younger to middle-aged to older conversational partners. For our purposes, an upshot of this research is the finding that intergenerational conversations involving young and middle-aged persons are relatively rare and subject to the same stereotyping effects experienced by older persons.

So the first task of this chapter is to look beyond the stereotypes of middle age, to answer in a clear-eyed way the question: *What does it mean to be middle-aged and living in the U.S. during this period of history?* Initially I answer this question by plumbing the depths of demographic databases, digging for data on rates of divorce, the onset of disease, employment trends, and other measures of the quality of midlife.

Then the chapter moves to the primary topic of this book, the experience of marriage (and other committed relationships) during the middle stage of the lifecourse. In Chapters 4–7, we hear what the couples themselves have to say. Here, I explore what the *research* has to say about couples who are jointly navigating the midlife landscape. These partners have been together for decades, yet many are reworking the relationship in response to new opportunities and challenges. Previously, Doug Kelley and I have characterized these as "centerstage" marriages, in part because many couples' interests return to frontstage after years spent backstage while their kids were the stars of the show (Waldron & Kelley, 2009). But the metaphor also applies to couples who are not parents. It recognizes that couples' taken-for-granted assumptions and practices may be pushed into the spotlight, scrutinized for their relevance as partners encounter the changing circumstances described above. As we will see, couples often view this center stage of marriage as both different and similar to their early years together. Some report that lessons learned over the first decades of practice have "protective" effects, leaving them well-prepared to perform their relationships at midlife, even when life goes off-script, adversity is encountered, and improvisation is required (see Chapter 4). Others report that relational habits—well-worn scripts and familiar roles—are insufficient given current realities. They find that new roles must be learned, scripts adjusted, and supportive audiences must be sought. To a greater or lesser degree these midlife actors reinvent their relationships, finding ways to cope (Chapter 5) and even grow (see Chapter 6) in response to new constraints and changing conditions.

Against this backdrop, what do we already know about these midlife couples? What developmental tasks do they face? How do couples themselves tell the story of their middle years together? And what does the social science research say? Which factors contribute to martial satisfaction and which work against it? How does the experience of midlife marriage vary by gender; race, ethnicity, and culture; sexual orientation, or socioeconomic status? In what ways do the relational practices change or stay the same as couples navigate the middle decades together? What are the "turning points," the watershed moments that alter the trajectory of midlife unions? These are some of the many questions addressed in this chapter.

The Demographic Imperative

One reason to study the relationships of middle aged persons is their sheer ubiquity. With so many Americans experiencing midlife at this point in our history, it seems a good time to learn more about them and the lives they are living. Table 1.1 lists some basic demographic data on midlife Americans, presented as percentages. When combined with other findings they helped me answer the questions below.

Table 1.1. Demographics of middle aged Americans.

Variable	Percentage (%)
Marital Status	
Married	82.2
Divorced	19.7
Gender	
Female	51
Male	49
Race/Ethnicity	
White	88.4
Black/African American	11.7
Asian	04.5
Native American/Alaskan	01.0
Native Hawaiian/Pacific Islander	<0.01
Multiple categories	01.1
Hispanic*	10.6
Sexual orientation	
Heterosexual	97.3
Lesbian or Gay	01.8
Bisexual	0.004

*Overlaps with other categories.

How Many People Are We Talking About?

According to the U.S. Census Bureau (2013) report on the age and sex composition of the population, 81,937,000 Americans were 40 to 64 years old in 2013. Of these, roughly 67,375,000 (82%) were married. Another 16,222,000 (19.7%) were divorced. So, being married at midlife is quite common. And it is apparently worth repeating. Data provided by the Pew Charitable trust show that Americans of middle age are more likely to remarry than those of earlier or older ages. For those in the 45–54 age group the number who married again was 63%. For 55 to 64 year olds, the number was 67%.

What About Their Kids?

The Gallup organization (2016) reports that middle-aged Americans have on average 2.5 children. Estimates of "boomerang" children are harder to come by. But the Pew Charitable Trust (2016) reports that in 2010 21% of adults aged 25–34 lived in a multigenerational household. Due to difficult economic circumstances and declining job opportunities, it is likely that number grew in the years after 2010.

How Diverse Are They?

Based on the 2010 census, 81.4% of middle-aged Americans identify as white. Another 11.7% identified as black or African American and 4.5% identified as Asian. Native Americans and Native Alaskans accounted for less than 1% of this group, as did Native Hawaiians/Pacific Islanders. A little over 1% identified with multiple ethnicities. Hispanic-identifying people constituted 10.6% of the total. These numbers look much different for younger Americans who are far more likely to identify as Hispanic or multi-ethnic.

Women slightly outnumber men. The U.S. census projected that in 2015, middle-aged women numbered 41,013,523, or 51% of this segment of the population. At 43,052,457, men counted as 49% of the middle aged population.

In terms of sexual orientation, the Centers for Disease Control (2016) report that in 2013 97% of middle aged Americans identify as heterosexual on the National Health Interview Survey. Another 1.8% identify as gay or lesbian, and 0.4% as bisexual.

How Healthy Are They?

Midlife is a time when certain health conditions become more common. This section addresses just a few of the most recognizable illnesses. One of those *is hypertension*. The CDC estimates that roughly 20% of white men in the 40–49 age range have been diagnosed with high blood pressure. The number doubles in the 50–59 age group, with 40% diagnosed. The numbers for women are 10% and 35% respectively. *Diabetes* is another chronic condition that becomes more common at midlife. As of 2014 there were roughly 13.4 million (16.2%) of Americans aged 45–64 living with diabetes (Centers for Disease Control, 2016). For men prostate cancer becomes a concern as midlife progresses, according to the U.S. government's cancer.gov website (2016). Roughly 9.5% of new cases are diagnosed among men aged 45–54 years. That number increases to 32.9% among those who are 55–64 years old. For women, the incidence of breast cancer increases over time. Cancer.gov reports that 21.3% of new diagnoses involve 45–54 year olds and 25.7% of new breast cancer patients are 55–64 years old.

Cardiovascular disease is also common at midlife. In the age group of 40–59 years old, 40.5% of men exhibit symptoms, according to the American Heart Association (2016). For women of the same age, the number is 35%. Heart attack risk is another consideration. In the age group 55–65 years, 12.5% of men and 6.0% of women are at risk for heart attack.

Finally, death becomes a reality at midlife. Working from 2013 data, the CDC (2016) indicates that the rate of death per 100,000 people more than *quadruples* in the midlife period, from 41,752 for the 40–44 year age group to 185,146 for those 60–64 years old. What do middle-aged people die from? For Americans 45–64 years old, the top ten causes of death are:

- Cancer—30.9%
- Heart disease—20.9%
- Other—20.1%
- Unintentional injuries—7.3%
- Chronic liver disease and cirrhosis—4.0%
- Chronic lower respiratory disease (CLRD)—4.0%*
- Diabetes—3.7%
- Stroke—3.3%
- Suicide—3.1%
- Septicemia—1.5%
- Influenza and pneumonia—1.4%

How Do Their Finances Look?

According to the U.S. Bureau of Labor Statistics (2016), the unemployment rate as of June 2016 for 35–44 year-olds was 3.7% and for 45–64 year-olds it was 3.5%. These numbers come in below the national average, which has hovered around 5.0%. Interestingly, the same report indicates that 80% of people over the age of 45 have considered changing their career, but only 6% actually did! Household income levels are relatively high among 44–64 year olds. Financial analyst Douglas Short (2015) examined trends in the U.S. census report for 2014. With household income in 2014 of $70,832, people aged 45–54 appear to be the highest earning demographic group. However, that group has seen a *decline* of real income of 12.4% since 1999. So middle-aged Americans may feel as if their fortunes are sinking rather than rising, even though they are quite well-off compared to those of other age groups.

So the economic picture is not all bright. In fact, the bureau reports that more than eleven million middle-aged people live below the poverty line. As noted by the Institute for Financial Literacy (2016), the median age of those who file for bankruptcy is now 45, squarely in middle age (2016). In 2010, 29% of those who filed for bankruptcy were between the ages of 45–54 and 18% were between the ages of 55–64. The most common reasons for filing bankruptcy are medical expenses, injury, and illness. Other explanations: overextension of credit, unexpected expenses, reduction of income, and job loss. In contrast, just 9% of bankruptcy filers were older than 65.

On a more positive note, the 2010 U.S. census indicates that 70% of 45–54 year olds own their own home. That number rises to 75.4% in the age 55–64 year age range. However, it appears that homeownership rates for middle-aged persons dropped more than other age groups during the recent recession.

For at least some middle-agers, retirement becomes a financial priority as the years pass. For the well-off retirement dreams may soon become realities. For others, retirement is an unwelcome event, forced upon them by illness or unexpected job loss. Still others will never be able to afford retirement. And an increasingly prominent group of middle-aged people just don't want to retire, at least in the traditional sense of that word. They prefer to stay employed, albeit with fewer work hours and more scheduling flexibility. In responding to a Heartland Monitor Poll (2011), 68% of "near retirees" expected to work in retirement with nearly half doing so out of financial necessity.

Atlantic Monthly business writer Ann Boschma (2015) reviewed data from a more recent Heartland Monitor Poll, reporting that nearly half of people

under the age of 50 express optimism that they will be able to afford retirement before the age of 65. That number drops to around 41 for people in
the 50–59 age range. Only 29% of older people feel optimistic that they will
retire. Interestingly, student debt seems to factor in this optimism equation.
Younger people are most burdened by long-term student debt but their parents
are sometimes on the hook as well. In order to pay off the debt, some middle-aged parents are delaying retirement.

All of this begs the question—Are middle-aged couples ready, in the
financial sense, to retire? Among the financial experts, the consensus seems
to be "no," given that the average American should have saved $1,000,000 to
fund a comfortable, lengthy retirement (Motley Fool, 2016). How much have
they saved? The average couple in their 50s has accumulated only $117,000,
while those is their 60s average $172,000. Of course, these numbers are influ-
enced by the reality that many couples have absolutely *zero* retirement savings. Their current income merely covers their expenses.

How Educated Are They?

U.S. census (2015) estimates for 2015 indicated that roughly 36% of Americans aged 40–44 years had attained at least a four-year college degree. For
those in the latter stages of middle age (ages 60–64) that number was around
32.6%. Changes in the economy combined with changing personal goals,
encourage some middle-aged persons couples to return to school. How many?
Data from the National Student Clearinghouse (2012) indicated that 17%
of all college students were over the age of 35. By 2020, that number was
expected to rise to 19%. Although many of these students are part-time, the
report noted that 34% of students over age 40 were enrolled full time.

What Does It All Mean?

The reader will understandably draw mixed conclusions from this dive into
the sea of demographic data. We see that many middle-aged Americans are
relatively well-employed, financially comfortable, and still married. However, they may be experiencing significant anxiety as incomes drop, retirement looms, and certain health conditions strike. Relatively few are seeking
new career fields. Perhaps that is one explanation for income declines. Yet, it
appears that more are returning to or reentering college, a sign of that they
may be adapting to changing circumstances. A significant number of midlife

couples have adult offspring living at home and some are helping their kids pay college debt. Compared to younger age groups, middle-aged Americans are certainly less diverse. But as younger adults progress into midlife, that will change too. Taken together these observations suggest that stability is giving way to change. As we turn our attention to the marriages of midlife people, we will learn more about how these couples are holding up.

Midlife Marriage: What the Research Says

I begin this exploration of the scholarly literature by first situating midlife as a unique developmental period, one that has received considerable attention in the work of such renowned developmental theorists as Erik Erikson and Robert Levinson. It is certainly true that earlier stages of life have more often been the focus of developmental psychologists, probably because childhood and adolescence are times of rapid and highly-noticeable change along such dimensions as social cognition, relationships with peers and family, and moral reasoning. Nonetheless, midlife plays a prominent role in most frameworks—a recognition that it is a time of growth and adaptation. As backdrop for this discussion, it is important to note that midlife is defined not merely by the *number of years* that have passed in a person's life. Time is certainly a factor, but developmental milestones can be more meaningful markers of this passage. Among them might be the "launching" of adult offspring, the assumption of mentoring roles, and achieving a degree of stability and satisfaction in ones work. Of course, even as middle-aged people (and couples) encounter these experiences, they may also repeat milestones more typically experienced earlier or later in the lifecourse. They may marry for the first time or have children. Or they may retire early or become grandparents. All of this is to say that the experiences of middle-aged couples can be both similar to, and divergent from, their peers.

The (Developmental) Tasks They Perform

Development can be conceived in terms of stages or tasks. The first approach assumes a temporal sequencing grounded in maturation and the normative events of the lifecourse, where the completion of one stage is typically a prerequisite for the other. Task models emphasize the cognitive and social work that must be completed if people are to grow and mature and find satisfaction in life. Tasks needn't be completed in sequence, but as with the models presented below, certain kinds of psychosocial tasks become more or less relevant during eras of the life course.

Erikson's theory of psychosocial development

In what may be the most prominent framing of midlife development, Erikson argues that this period of life is defined by generativity or stagnation (Erikson, 1959, 1963; Erikson & Erikson, 1997). Generativity is one's concern for, and willingness to invest in, the well-being of future generations (see also McAdams, 2013). It suggests a capacity to expand one's view beyond the needs of self. Having reached a point of stability and satisfaction in career, finances, family life, and self-understanding, the middle-aged person is presumed to be more willing and able to invest in others. For Erikson, this investment is expressed in childrearing and perhaps grandparenting activities. But generativity also comes in the form of mentoring younger colleagues, accepting positions of civic leadership, and increased help-giving. Having met basic needs and achieved a certain sense of security, some middle-aged persons seek relationships and activities that make life meaningful. They may seek their "calling" and be willing to take some risks (e.g. leaving a familiar job or marriage) in an effort to seek significance.

In contrast, Erikson's (1959) description of stagnation suggests a "hunkering down" at midlife, a preference for security, comfort, and self-gratification. Stagnating persons are concerned with relieving their own dissatisfaction and consolidating resources. They may be aware of their own relative lack of productivity earlier in life but are unwilling to invest in self-development. They are risk-averse, may avoid change, and fail to see the value of investing in new relationships. They are unlikely to find meaning in mentoring or community leadership activities.

Erikson's dichotomy can be criticized for painting midlife with such broad strokes, and certainly many midlives are marked by elements of both stagnation and generativity. One can easily imagine for example, stagnation in one life context (e.g. marriage) and generativity in another (e.g., career). In fact Erikson argued that development involved acknowledgment of the *tension* between generativity and stagnation and an active working out of the balance between them. Erikson's formulation remains broadly influential as a roadmap of successful progression though the lifecourse. When extended beyond individuals to midlife couples, we can see the tensions between generativity and stagnation being worked out in relational practices and conflicts. For example, some midlife partners jointly seek new shared activities and encourage the seeking out of new friends. In contrast others express a comfort with familiar activities while despairing over the loss of friendships developed during their years of active parenting (Waldron & Kelley, 2009). In this sense, the developmental orientations proposed by Erikson are (in part) enacted, reinforced, or negotiated via interaction. So it seems that our effort to understand the challenges and opportunities posed by midlife relationships will be enhanced by examining the ways in which partners mutually-support (or inhibit) generativity and stagnation.

Levinson's "seasons of life"

In 1978, psychologist Daniel Levinson and several colleagues reported the results of a study based on extensive interviews designed to document exhaustively the lifecourse of the American male (Levinson, Darrow, Klein, Levinson, & McKee, 1978). Much later, he would publish the results of a similar study of American women (Levinson, 1996). Levinson intended to expand the seminal work of Erikson by looking beyond the psychosocial element of development and by offering a finer-grained assessment of stages and transitional phases. Often consolidated under the term "seasons of life theory."

Levinson's work has generated some criticism, first for its early neglect of the female lifecourse and second for its failure to account for the role that cultural differences and generational change might play in determining the presence, order, and importance of certain developmental events. The theory is highly detailed, and perhaps guilty of over-specifying the experiences typical of narrow age-bands, such as the period between 50 and 55 years of age. Despite these limitations, his body of work deserves our attention because it sheds light on the developmental challenges of midlife, which Levinson himself apparently struggled to resolve (Newton, 1994).

Levinson viewed development as a changing set of relationships connecting the individual with other people, work, and social institutions. It was during ages 40–45, he claimed, that the transition to midlife occurred, a time when these connections must be amended to reflect impending midlife changes, such as declining physical health or changed roles in the workforce. During the midlife transition, some aspects of one's youthful identity and activity must be left behind and others significantly altered. This winnowing and changing process was a foundation of wisdom. Moreover, discord in relationships should be resolved he thought, so one can transition to the more peaceful, less conflictual period of midlife. The inability to complete these tasks resulted in a "midlife crisis." The timing, intensity, and ubiquity of the midlife crisis has been questioned in subsequent years but the term conveyed what Levinson thought he heard in his interviews—that a successful transition to midlife required great, and sometimes unsettling, changes.

For Levinson, the resolution of certain "polarities" defined middle age. One of these involved destruction and creation. One must make peace with, and perhaps amends for, destructive activities of the past. At the same time, echoing Erikson, Levinson saw a successful midlife as one that created value for others even as the transitioning adult found increased satisfaction in changing identity. Another polarity involved tensions between what Levinson believed to be masculine and feminine approaches to life. As he saw things, women transitioned to become more masculine; that is, more assertive and autonomous. In contrast men were more likely to embrace traditionally feminine qualities such as empathy and connectedness. Engagement and separation made another pair of opposites. Levinson's interviews suggested that middle-aged women were engaging the wider world though expanded involvement in the workplace and enlarging social networks. His male interviewees described a curbing of externally-oriented ambition and an increasing focus on self-understanding.

The middle stage of life was further partitioned in this seasons-of-life framework. The early years may involve considerable adjustment and acceptance while the late 50s can be a time of stability, fulfillment, and life enhancement. As older age approaches however, the physical realities of aging and the prospect of leaving the workforce can prompt new reflection and identity work. As one's identity as an older person becomes a reality relationships with people, work, and social institutions must once again be renegotiated. Levinson's probing of the different eras of midlife proved useful in analyzing the interviews upon which this book is based. Some of the couples were young enough (early- to mid-forties) to be in the midst of transition, whereas others were solidly ensconced in midlife, while still others were in their 60s, aging to the point where the term "middle age" was losing its relevance. Still others had now aged well beyond their middle years of life, so they were uniquely positioned to reflect on the full range of Levinson's micro-stages and polarities. The inclusion of these older (and younger) couples increases my confidence that our findings are not limited solely to a certain cohort—those that are currently ensconced in middle-age. The range of views helps us determine the degree to which some middle age experiences are fleeting phenomena, tied to a particular moment in the development of the larger culture, and others are experienced consistently at certain points in the lifecourse.

As with Erikson's (1959) framework, Levinson's thinking left me wondering how couples, not just individuals, negotiated the polarities of midlife. Several of them resonate clearly with my own observations. In interviews that formed the basis of our 2008 book, *Communicating Forgiveness*, Douglas Kelley and I saw middle-aged partners struggling with what we called the justice-mercy dialectic. Having experienced destructive patterns of behavior in the past, some midlife pairs described efforts to be merciful—to "put the past in the past," let go of long-held grudges, and invest their efforts in creating a new and better relationship. Others appeared locked in destructive cycles of revenge fueled by unresolved feelings of blame and preoccupation with a painful past. The communication practices that enact forgiveness may be one of the means by which Levinson's destruction versus creation polarity is resolved. And at the risk of revealing too much about the coming chapters, our interviews yield considerable support for Levinson's general idea (if not his specific observations) that personal definitions of masculinity and femininity are often renegotiated at midlife.

Duvall's family stages

Development is not just an individual matter. Couples and families change over the lifecourse, as they travel together (sometimes more intertwined, sometimes less). E. R. Duvall (1977) proposed a model of family development, focusing on the tasks that families must complete at various periods of the life course. Two of those are unique to midlife. The first is "rebuilding the marriage relationship." How do couples and the larger family system work together to redefine the marriage, as child-rearing tasks become less central and the partners begin to reevaluate roles, routines, and the allocation of their shared resources? Thinking of the family as the unit of analysis is advantageous because we can see that partners' efforts to re/define their relationship could be influenced by such factors as the success of their offspring in becoming independent or offspring support for parents' efforts to explore other dimensions of adult life through such actions as returning to school or relocating to a new community. The availability of role models in the larger family could be another factor. How did the older generation of parents adapt (or not) during midlife?

The other midlife task is maintaining kin ties with both older and younger family members. Midlife partners may be challenged by the geographic distance that separates them from offspring or grandchildren (Bangerter & Waldron, 2014). Mastering certain communication technologies may facilitate this task. Generational distance can also complicate matters, as children adopt values, lifestyles, or spiritual practices that differentiate them from their parents and potentially complicate the relationship. Examples might be the practice of an unfamiliar religious faith or the enactment of nontraditional gender identities. Connections with aging parents also fit here, as midlife couples negotiate over how to support mothers or fathers who become ill or dependent in some way. Should mom move into our house? How will we support dad now that mom has passed away? How will the couple share the duties of caregiving? These and other kin-keeping questions arise at midlife.

Researchers have tried to identify the practices that foster successful completion of the two midlife tasks (Huber, Navarro, Womble, & Mumme, 2010). Drawing on the family adaptation model (Drummond, Kysela, McDonald, & Query, 2002), Huber and colleagues examined the role of three protective characteristics of families thought to make couples less vulnerable to the stressors of midlife. These include social support, adaptive appraisals, and compensating experiences. The first of these includes access to various kinds of support (e.g., emotional, informational) in the family network. The second involves a capacity to think constructively in the face of challenging circumstances, to include thoughts of self-efficacy, acceptance of reality, forming positive expectations, and trusting oneself and others to prevail. The third factor, compensating experiences, included taking action that fostered positive emotions, clarified/or redefined problems, and moved the family toward a solution. Results of a survey study of midlife couples indicated that all three factors, but especially adaptive appraisal and compensating actions, were associated with successful performance of Duvall's (1977) marriage rebuilding and kin-keeping tasks.

Duvall's model, although proposed in the 1970s holds up fairly well today. Certainly, as we examined the challenges described by midlife couples (Chapter 3), we saw evidence that in 2016, many families are working through these developmental tasks. This line of research cued our research team to the potential importance of the larger family in shaping responses to midlife stressors and to the potential role played by appraisal, compensation, and social support.

The Stories They Tell

In the 1970s and early 1980s, researchers were questioning the stage and task models of development and encouraging a renewed focus on the subjective meanings that people associated with their lives, the stories they told about their past (Cohler, 1982). They argued that it was in the constructing of narratives about their lives that people found integrative themes, expressed their evolving identities, found and kindled a sense of purpose, and imagined a trajectory for the future (McAdams, 2014). By midlife, people have accumulated considerable experience and a complicated life history that lends itself to rich storytelling. Their life stories are expanding and deepening with chapters that might include "early life," "the school years," "relationships and marriage," "careers," "parenting," "the empty nest" and possibly "health challenges," "divorce," "remarriage" or "stepfamily life." For some, moments of rapid change may standout against a background of relative stability. Others may not perceive such obvious turning points, but rather gradual changes as one stage of life eases into another.

These life stories interest clinicians and researchers because they reveal much about what is considered meaningful to those who have reached the midpoint of a complicated and evolving lifecourse (Adler, 2012; Dunn, 2003). They shape individual identities and their telling is one means by which other family members are socialized (Gregg, 1991). By extension, relational narratives yield clues about the forces that shaped a marriage and the ways in which it is changing (or not) now, at midlife. The story of a long relationship may be interpreted as a trajectory, one that will carry a couple into their old age together or lead them to different version of the future. For all of these reasons, I take some space here to review what we can learn from studies of the stories middle-aged people tell.

One prominent line of research links storytelling to generativity (McAdams, 2013; McAdams & Aubin, 1992), Erikson's (1963) notion that at midlife healthy psychosocial development stems from a willingness to invest in the well-being of future generations. McAdams and his colleagues have accumulated evidence to support the idea that the life stories of highly generative, and apparently more satisfied, persons are qualitatively different from those who are less generative ("stagnant" in Erikson's terms). Grounded in lengthy interviews designed to prompt the telling of life narratives, this research convinced McAdams that the theme of *redemption* was prominent in the stories of the most satisfied and productive middle-aged persons. These stories have in common an experience of adversity that severely challenged the teller, who nonetheless managed to prevail and "make good."

In recent work, McAdams (2013) has expanded on this idea, suggesting that generative persons told life narratives featuring a prototypical *redemptive self*, featuring

> five independent psychological themes that, taken together, characterize this quint-essentially American story about how to live a good life: (a) *early advantage* (the protagonist is singled out for positive distinction), (b) *sensitivity to suffering* (the protagonist is moved by the suffering of other people or by oppression, inequality, or some other social ill), (c) *moral steadfastness* (a strong moral framework guides the protagonist's actions), (e) *redemption sequences* (negative events turn positive), and (e) *prosocial goals* (the protagonist expressly aims to improve the lives of other people or society more generally). (McAdams & Guo, 2015, p. 476)

In a study of stories related by 157 middle-aged persons (ages 55–57, 63.6% female) McAdams and Guo found that each of these dimensions was positively associated with measures of generativity, public service commitment, and psychological well-being. They were negatively associated with depression.

Several explanations can be offered for this connection between storytelling and midlife adaptation (McAdams, 2014). First, these redemption narratives are a *resource* as new challenges are encountered at midlife. They provide evidence that a person (or couple) have encountered and overcome adversity and their telling may stoke resolve, confidence, and hope. In this way, narrative is a way of enacting relational resilience (see Lucas & Buzzanell, 2012). Second, narratives can be recast at midlife, helping midlife couples reimagine the future in a way that is liberating or motivating. A recently reported intervention helps couples "re-purpose" the empty nest by creating a new life story, one that directs attention away from role loss towards possibilities for growth and fulfillment (Mount & Moas, 2015). Third, such stories may motivate people to be generative. In turn generativity leads to satisfaction at midlife. The redemptive self has been blessed by an advantage of some kind (a good upbringing, supportive friends, good health) but realizes that others may not be so lucky. He or she has experienced serious adversity but managed to turn negative circumstances into positive ones (McAdams, Reynolds, Lewis, Patten, & Bowman, 2001). For these reasons, the middle-aged person feels gratitude and a determination to make things better for others. They may feel a sense of "mission" that guides these efforts to "give back" (McAdams, 2014).

Generativity is associated with satisfaction and productivity, but it also requires commitment (McAdams, Diamond, & Mansfield, 1997). Generative people engage themselves as mentors, caregivers, leaders. They may be active in community, church, volunteer organizations or their extended family. All of these involvements can yield frustration. As McAdams (2014) observes, "Generativity is hard work. You need a good story to get you through" (p. 64). This then is the third connection between narrative and midlife adaptation. Stories sustain generative commitments. They provided a rationale for persisting, a fortification of ones identity as a person who wants to invest in the next generation.

This work on narrative identity cued me to look for redemptive themes as midlife couples talked about their marriages. Drawing once again on McAdams (2013) I wondered if couples might offer variations on one of the four "master narratives" of redemption common to American culture. These include themes of *atonement* (from sin to salvation), *upward mobility* (from rags to riches), *liberation* from oppression (racism, sexism, homophobia, etc.), and recovery (addiction or abuse). Breaking from McAdams, I wanted to consider that these might be collectively-constructed tales, with partners sharing the task of telling a story that featured them both in key roles and relational scenes.

The Nature of their Bonds

Thus far I have painted midlife marriage in the broad strokes of developmental tasks and storytelling themes. But the literature also yields a finer-grained, if highly-fragmented portrayal of the marital lives of the middle-aged. I am grateful to my former students Daniel Kelley and Qun Lu for helping me track down and synthesize this literature, a collection of data-based studies on various aspects of these marriages. I note in advance that the literature has yet to accumulate sufficiently to support many firm conclusions. And much of the literature is becoming dated, as American culture changes in ways that inevitably shape the contours of both marriage and midlife. To mention just a few of these trends:

- Emerging communication technologies and social media are offering new opportunities for parents and their adult offspring to remain connected, although they may (as mentioned above) also promote generational stratification.
- Economic upheaval in recent years has increased the rate of "boomeranging children" and the degree to which parents and offspring are economically intertwined.

- The children of midlife parents are marrying later and fewer are choosing to marry at all.
- The nature of retirement is changing with fewer midlife persons aspiring to leave the workforce as midlife transitions to older age.

For all of these reasons I report the existing literature succinctly, focusing on areas of research that have received more than passing attention and the studies that prove most useful in helping us understand the changes, challenges, and opportunities experienced by midlife couples.

Research on changes

A prevalent topic of research has been the transitions shared by midlife couples. And among those the most researched is the "empty nest." In a recent review Bouchard (2014) nicely integrates the various studies published in recent decades on this family phenomenon. The author searched the literature for synonymous terms, such as "post-parental," "post-maternity," "post-parenthood," "launching of offspring," "launching phase," and "leaving-home trajectory" in research data bases. According to Bouchard, the earliest studies were conducted in the 1950s but the topic received increased attention in the 1970s, as the lifespan increased and the post-parental period lengthened. One result was increasing dissatisfaction with the empty nest metaphor because of its negative conations (hence the use of the equally unappealing "post-parental"). Researchers came to distinguish the *launching* phase from the *empty-nest* phase, with the former describing the period when offspring are preparing to leave or experimenting with independent living. In the launching phase, the oldest offspring may have left home, but younger siblings remain with their parents. The launching phase ends when the last child leaves home.

Bouchard (2014) concludes that nest leaving is typically voluntary, with most parents expecting it to happen between the ages of 18 and 25. However, the average age of leaving has been rising in recent years due changes in the economy which make it harder for younger people to find jobs with sufficient income. A concomitant trend is the tendency of families to be more comfortable with delayed independence. Traditionally, demographic data indicate that women leave the house before men. This is mostly due to the tendency of women to marry earlier, but this trend may be changing. Offspring from larger families and those from step-families tend to leave earlier. The majority of offspring that do leave the family home end up living relatively close to their parents.

The effects of the empty nest can be explained by the two theoretical constructs of role loss and role strain/relief. Bouchard's (2014) review indicates that parents in general, and mothers in particular, experience a sense of loss because their sense of accomplishment has been for decades partially-sustained by parenting. What has become known as *empty-nest syndrome* is heightened when alternative roles are unavailable. In contrast a role strain perspective predicts an improvement in parental well-being because the presence of children increases exposure to caregiving stressors and challenges of work-life balance. It appears that both role loss and role relief are reported by midlife parents, with some parents experiencing both.

A narrative-based intervention "re-purposing the empty nest" helps midlife parents reframe the end of parenting by integrating their "parent" narrative more fully with the larger story of their life (Mount & Moas, 2015). The goal is to help parents renew their sense of purpose. Some parents experience this without intervention, experiencing it as a natural result of new experiences at home, at work, or in civic life. Others need assistance in reconnecting with latent qualities and reimagining themselves in a productive and satisfying role. The authors present the case of Cindy, a 45-year-old mother of two adult offspring who had recently left home. Cindy lacked social connections and was laboring in an unsatisfying part-time job. In therapy Cindy constructed a new visual representation of her life path, one that expressed hopes and plans for a satisfying midlife and included a chapter entitled "Time for ME."

For many couples another life transition involves caregiving for aging parents. The caregiving roles can be satisfying, but as one study established, it can also be a source of martial distress (Lee, Zarit, Rovine, Birditt, & Fingerman, 2011). Lee and colleagues assessed the effects of caregiving on the relational satisfaction of middle-aged partners (40–60 years old) living in the northeastern U.S. Each couple had at least one adult offspring. Notable for its significant sample size, the study involved hour-long interviews with 335 married participants and 287 of their spouses. Participants were asked to rate their martial satisfaction and to indicate how often they provided parents with six types of support: emotional, practical assistance, socializing, advice, financial support and talking about daily events. The amount of support received from parents was also assessed. The results suggested (predictably) that couples with more living parents reported more support giving activity. When totaled, the amount of support given by the two partners showed no effects on marital satisfaction, a finding the researchers credit to the resources available at middle age and the intermittent nature of support provided by most couples in this age group. However, spouses who gave (and received) more parental support reported lower marital satisfaction compared to their partners. The results support the idea that midlife brings with it a degree of caregiving stress that might strain a marriage. But the authors also suggest that less-satisfied partners may offer and receive more support from parents, an interpretation that associates caregiving with relational coping (the subject of Chapter 5).

Research on challenges

Researchers have examined threats to the stability of midlife marriages. The return of departed children ("boomerang kids") is one area that has received considerable attention (Bouchard, 2014). The return of adult children can be disruptive and tension between parents, returning offspring, and younger off-spring is not uncommon. But, such returns may not be as disruptive as might be imagined, especially when the parents expect it to happen, cultural norms support it, and the family negotiates expectations (Waldron & Kelley, 2009). However, Bouchard noted some evidence that couples experience a reduction of sexual activity after children return home and some indication that parents report a reduction in positive interactions. Fathers are apparently more affected than mothers, as they reported greater changes in mood in at least one study. Bouchard notes that good research is relatively scant, especially when it comes to the differential effects experienced in nontraditional families, across cultural subgroups, and between mothers and fathers. Looking beyond the boomerang effect, relationships with adult offspring can also be a chronic source of stress. A study of "intergenerational ambivalence" showed that unsatisfying connections increased depressive symptoms and decreased happiness for both wives and husbands. These effects can persist over long periods of the lifecourse (Kiecolt, Blieszner, & Savla, 2011).

However, factors other than relationships with offspring can disrupt midlife marriages. Cutrona and colleagues investigated threats to relational stability among heterosexual African American couples (Cutrona, Russell, Burzette, Bryant, & Wesner, 2011). A unique feature of the study was its requirement that each couple have at least one elementary-school-age child remaining at home. Drawing on a vulnerability-stress–adaptation model of marriage, the authors described several influences on marital functioning. *Enduring vulnerabilities* are characteristics that influence a couple's susceptibility to stressful life events, such as sustained poverty or chronic poor health. *Stressful events* are current episodes of adversity, such as job loss or unexpected expenses. Enduring vulnerabilities intensify the effects of these episodic factors because they drain away coping resources. The *adaptive processes* a couple uses to manage stressors, such as problem solving conversations, will influence the stability of the relationship.

The authors hypothesized that financial strain (enduring factor) would decrease relationship stability at midlife. However, they expected the effects to be mediated by the quality of the relationship, an indicator that the couple has developed adaptive processes. They predicted that current stressors would erode stability but expected that couples who were married (rather than cohabitating) would experience more stability, as would those who reported higher levels of religious involvement. In this longitudinal study, all predictor variables were administered at Wave 1 when the ages of most participants ranged between 37 and 40 years. The primary outcome variable was relationship stability, which was assessed 5 years after the Wave 1 interview.

Results indicated that 75% of the couples remained intact over the five year period. Being married and having both biological parents in the home were associated positively with stability, while financial strain correlated negatively with stability. Female perceptions of relationship quality and religiosity and male education and income were significantly associated with relationship stability. This study is significant because it demonstrates that enduring financial hardship can take a relational toll as midlife progresses. It also hints at factors that promote relationship resilience, some of which may vary by gender. These include engagement with religiosity and education.

What other challenges do midlife couples face? One study queried midlife couples, finding differential partner relationships with offspring and sexuality (along with financial stressors) were the most-reported problems (Henry & Miller, 2004). In contrast, differences in values, commitment, spiritual matters, and violence were least common. These results were little changed when gender, remarriage, and length of marriage were considered. Among these challenges, sexuality stands out because it has been characterized as both a challenge of midlife (Lodge & Umberson, 2012) and a predictor of relational happiness (see below Heiman et al., 2011). The first of these sources interviewed middle-aged (50–69 years) and older (70–86 years) married partners about changes in their sex lives. Partners were interviewed separately. Physical changes often affected the sex lives of midlife couples and for some this caused distress.

Later life couples appeared to have adapted to these changes and tended to emphasize the importance of emotional intimacy in their sex lives. Moreover, midlife husbands and wives experienced marital sex differently, whereas older husbands and wives offered more congruent reports. Midlife women were distressed when their partners showed curtailed interest in sex, some-times attributing this to age-related unattractiveness. In short, this study con-firms that sexuality can be a source of midlife adversity, one that women and men may experience differently. These differences may reflect the internaliza-tion of gendered stereotypes about the attractiveness of the aging body.

Researchers have studied how couples match on various personal qualities in an effort to identify those who are likely to sustain relationships through the turbulence of midlife. One study grouped couples based on degree to which they matched on gender-linked attributes of instrumentality and expressive-ness (Helms, Proulx, Klute, McHale, & Crouter, 2006). The upshot of this research seems to be that extreme gender-typing is a risk factor. Androgynous midlife couples reported higher levels of martial satisfaction. Research has identified other enduring vulnerabilities. For example, it appears that insecure attachment can have long term effects, manifesting in marital distress during midlife (Hollist & Miller, 2005). For both men and women, insecure attach-ment styles were negatively associated with marital quality, even among long-term couples. The instability that characterizes insecure attachment may be an enduring stressor that makes couples more vulnerable to midlife challenges.

Research on opportunities

Research suggests that midlife creates opportunities as well as challenges for couples. With prolonged commitment and experience some couples may experience increased satisfaction. A relatively recent study of these matters was notable for its international scope (Heiman et al., 2011). The study is among the few to examine relational happiness and sexual satisfaction within a cross-cultural sample of middle-aged and older persons (range = 40–70 years; median = 55 years). The authors collected data from 200 couples in Brazil, Germany, Japan, Spain, and the U.S. to accumulate a sample size of 1000 people. Roughly 90% of the couples had children.

Participants were recruited by phone in the U.S., Germany, and Spain and then mailed questionnaires. In Brazil and Japan participation was solic-ited by in-person visits to households. The International Survey of Relationships (ISR) was employed, a multi-dimensional measure of demographics, health, mood, selected sexual history, sexuality behaviors and experiences over the past 4 weeks and 12 months. Participants rated their relational happiness and sexual satisfaction over the past 4 weeks. Differences between men and women were examined.

When survey responses were analyzed demographic data proved to be relatively unimportant in predicting happiness. Length of the relationships was predictive of happiness of both male and female partners. Those who had been together longest were most happy. Health status was a predictor, but only for men, who were more likely to report a happy relationship if they were healthy. However, measures of physical intimacy predicted relational happiness for men. In particular, those who valued their partner's orgasm were more likely to report relationship happiness. Frequent kissing and cuddling both increased the odds of relationship happiness by approximately three times. For women, no measure of physical intimacy was significantly predictive of relationship happiness.

In regards to sexual satisfaction, men with good health had an increase in sexual satisfaction. And some international differences were found. For example, Japanese men reported greater sexual satisfaction than American men. For men, physical intimacy measures and valuing one's partner's orgasm both positively impacted sexual satisfaction. Frequent kissing and cuddling were both important factors as well. Frequency of sex over the last 4 weeks increased sexual satisfaction in men as did measures of sexual functioning. For women, neither demographic nor health variables were associated with sexual satisfaction. However, frequent cuddling and kissing increased the self-reported sexual satisfaction of women. Sexual frequency over the past 4 weeks had a significant positive effect on women as well as did sexual functioning.

It is worth noting that relationship happiness and sexual satisfaction were significantly correlated in this study of (mostly) midlife couples. Frequent kissing and cuddling appeared to give equal satisfaction to both men and women, although men's happiness appeared to be more closely tied to physical intimacy. A key conclusion (for our purposes) is that the longer the duration of the marriage the greater marital satisfaction was found in both men and women.

Resilience-promoting practices of couples have been assessed for their effects on midlife marriages. Above I described the practices (e.g., adaptive appraisal) that facilitated performance of key midlife tasks, such as rebuilding the marital relationship (Huber et al., 2010). But the resilience of the larger family has been the focus of some studies. In a conceptual review, Black and Lobo (2008) defined family resilience as the capacity to experience warmth, support, and cohesion during times of hardship. Factors supporting family resilience included shared spirituality, flexibility, family communication, financial management, family time, shared recreation, routines and rituals, and external support networks.

In one analysis of low income families those that cultivated constructive communication, problem solving, and social support experienced more positive relational outcomes (Orthner, Jones-Sanpei, & Williamson, 2004). Indeed, the discourse practices cultivated by midlife parents, the metaphors they use, and the stories they tell, may promote resilience in the face of such challenges as job loss or economic hard times (Lucas & Buzzanell, 2012). These studies encouraged me to look closely at the metaphors midlife couples used when describing relationship adjustments (see Chapters 5 and 6).

As life progresses and couples make role adjustments, they may also experience a redistribution of power. For example a spouse who worked part-time or stayed at home as a fulltime caregiver may reenter the workforce, a move that might increase her or his economic influence in the relationship. A recently-reported longitudinal study documented the effects of power balancing on martial satisfaction at midlife (LeBaron, Miller, & Yorgason, 2014). The authors note that inequality in marital power has been linked to marital distress, divorce, and depression. The study analyzed data originally collected in 1969 and 1970. Participants were 175 female spouses of male medical students who were subsequently interviewed four different times during the 1969–2006 period. The average participant during the initial interview was 25.5 years old, had no children, and had been married for three years or less. One-hundred percent of the participants were Caucasian. Some of the data reported in 2014 were drawn from later interviews, when the women had been married for an average of 23.9 years. Marital power was measured using six survey items assessing the equality of power in the relationship and decision-making responsibilities. The results indicated that women in egalitarian marriages reported higher levels of concurrent happiness. They were also happier 15 years after the original measure was taken.

Conclusion

This review of the empirical research confirms what I concluded earlier from the demographic data. Midlife is a period of life when couples experience both stability and change, smooth sailing and exposure to bouts of adversity. Some types of stress may be unavoidable, such as caretaking for a parent or a downturn in financial fortunes. Others, such as discord concerning relationships with adult offspring and unequal sharing of power may be sidestepped as partners renegotiate relational practices and understandings. These adjustments may become necessary in other areas too, such as sexual intimacy and providing care for aging parents. Importantly, partners confront these forces not just as a couple, but as central players in larger family systems that may be more or less resilient.

The literature to date is suggestive, particularly to a scholar of family communication. There exists enough research to suggest that the capacity to negotiate roles, make sense of change, and reinterpret intimacy is particularly crucial at this time of life. Yet few communication researchers have made it their work to listen closely to couples at midlife, to develop a broad and deep understanding of the kinds of the relational practices that facilitate or hinder them. Reporting the results of that kind of listening is the primary purpose of this book.

References

Adler, J. M. (2012). Living into the story: Agency and coherence in a longitudinal study of narrative identity development and mental health over the course of psychotherapy. *Journal of Personality and Social Psychology, 102*, 367–389.

Bangerter, L., & Waldron, V. R. (2014). Turning points in long distance grandparent-grandchild relationships. *Journal of Aging Studies, 29*, 88–97.

Black, K., & Lobo, M. (2008). A conceptual review of family resilience factors. *Journal of Family Nursing, 14*, 33–55.

Boschma, A. (2015, June 23). How much do people think they'll need to retire? *Atlantic Monthly*. Retrieved from http://www.theatlantic.com/business/archive/2015/06/ideal-retirement-age-work/396464/

Bouchard, G. (2014). How do parents react when their children leave home? An integrative review. *Journal of Adult Development, 21*, 69–79.

Cohler, B. J. (1982). Personal narrative and life course. In P. B. Baltes & O. G. Brim (Eds.), *Life-span development and behavior* (Vol. 4, pp. 205–241). New York, NY: Academic Press.

Cutrona, C. E., Russell, D. W., Burzette, R. G., Bryant, C. M., & Wesner, K. A. (2011). Predicting relationship stability among midlife African American couples. *Journal of Consulting and Clinical Psychology, 79*(6), 814–825.

Drummond, J., Kysela, G. M., McDonald, L., & Query, B. (2002). The family adaptation model: Examination of dimensions and relations. *Canadian Journal of Nursing Research, 34*, 29–46.

Dunn, D. S. (2003). Teach me about your life: Narrative approaches to lives, meaning, and transitions. *Journal of Social and Clinical Psychology, 22*(5), 604–606.

Duvall, E. R. (1977). *Marriage and family development*. Philadelphia: Lippincott Williams & Wilkins.

Erikson, E. H. (1959). *Identity and the life cycle*. New York, NY: International Universities Press.

Erikson, E. H. (1963). *Childhood and society* (2nd ed.). New York, NY: W. W. Norton.

Erikson, E. H., & Erikson, J. M. (1997). *The life cycle completed: Extended version*. New York, NY: W. W. Norton.

Giles, H., Hajek C., Stoitsova, T., & Choi, C. W. (2010). Intergenerational communication satisfaction and age boundaries in Bulgaria and the United States. *Journal of Cross-Cultural Gerontology, 25*, 133–147. doi:10.1007/s10823-010-9114-x

Gregg, G. S. (1991). *Self-representation: Life narrative studies in identity and ideology*. Santa Barbara, CA: Greenwood Press.

Heiman, J. R., Long, J. S., Smith, S. N., Fisher, W. A., Sand, M. S., & Rosen, R. C. (2011). Sexual satisfaction and relationship happiness in midlife and older couples in five countries. *Archives of Sexual Behavior, 40*, 741–753.

Helms, H. M., Proulx, C. M., Klute, M. M., McHale, S. M., & Crouter, A. C. (2006). Spouses' gender-typed attributes and their links with marital quality: A pattern analytic. *Journal of Social and Personal Relationships, 23*(6), 843–864. doi:10.1177/0265407506068266

Henry, R. G., & Miller, R. B. (2004). Marital problems occurring in midlife: Implications for couples therapists. *The American Journal of Family Therapy, 32*, 405–417. doi:10.1080/01926180490455204

Hollist, C. S., & Miller, R. B. (2005, January). Perceptions of attachment style and marital quality in midlife marriage. *Family Relations, 54*(1), 46–57.

Huber, C. H., Navarro, R. L., Womble, M. W., & Mumme, F. L. (2010). Family resilience and midlife marital satisfaction. *The Family Journal: Counseling and Therapy for Couples and Families, 18*(2), 136–145. doi:10.1177/1066480710364477

Kiecolt, K. J., Blieszner, R., & Savla, J. (2011). Long-term influences of intergenerational ambivalence on midlife parents' psychological well-being. *Journal of Marriage and Family, 73*, 369–382. doi:10.1111/j. 1741-3737.2010.00812.x

LeBaron, C. D., Miller, R. B., & Yorgason, J. B. (2014). A longitudinal examination of women's perceptions of marital power and marital happiness in midlife marriages. *Journal of Couple and Relationship Therapy, 13*, 93–113.

Lee, J. E., Zarit, S. H., Rovine, M. J., Birditt, K. S., & Fingerman, K. L. (2011). Middle-aged couples' exchanges of support with aging parents: Patterns and association with marital satisfaction. *Gerontology, 58*, 88–96.

Levinson, D. (1996). *The seasons of a woman's life*. New York, NY: Random House.

Levinson, D., Darrow, C. N., Klein, E. B., Levison, M., & McKee, B. (1978). *The seasons of a man's life*. New York, NY: Knopf.

Lodge, A. C., & Umberson, D. (2012). All shook up: Sexuality of mid- to later-life married couples. *Journal of Marriage and Family, 74*, 428–443.

Lucas, K., & Buzzanell, P. M. (2012). Memorable messages of hard times: Constructing short- and long-term resiliences through family communication. *Journal of Family Communication, 12*, 189–208. doi:10.1080/15267431.2012.687196

McAdams, D. P. (2013). *The redemptive self: Stories Americans live by* (rev. ed.). New York, NY: Oxford University Press.

McAdams, D. P. (2014). The life narrative at midlife. *New Directions for Child and Adolescent Development, 145*, 57–69. doi:10.1002/cad.20067

McAdams, D. P., & Aubin, E. D. S. (1992). A theory of generativity and its assessment through self-report, behavioral acts, and narrative themes in autobiography. *Journal of Personality and Social Psychology, 62*(6), 1003–1015.

McAdams, D. P., Diamond, A., & Mansfield, E. (1997). Stories of commitment: The psychosocial construction of generative lives. *Journal of Personality and Social Psychology, 72*(3), 678–694.

McAdams, D. P., & Guo, J. (2015). Narrating the generative life. Psychological Science, 26, 475–483.

McAdams, D. P., Reynolds, J., Lewis, M., Patten, A. H., & Bowman, P. J. (2001). When bad things turn good and good things turn bad: Sequences of redemption and contamination in life narrative and their relation to psychosocial adaptation in midlife adults and in students. *Personality and Social Psychology Bulletin, 27*(4), 474–485.

McCann, R. M., Dailey, R. M., Giles, H., & Ota, H. (2005). Beliefs about intergenerational communication across the lifespan: Middle age and the roles of age stereotyping and respect norms. *Communication Studies, 56*, 293–311. doi:10.1080/10510970500319286

Mount, S. D., & Moas, S. (2015). Re-purposing the "empty nest." *Journal of Family Psychology, 26*(3), 247–252.

National Student Clearinghouse. (2012, April 19). *More than one-third of college students are over the age of 25* [press release]. Retrieved from http://www.studentclearinghouse.org

Newton, P. M. (1994). Daniel Levinson and his theory of adult development: A reminiscence and some clarifications. *Journal of Adult Development, 1*, 135. doi:10.1007/BF02260089

Orthner, D. K., Jones-Sanpei, H., & Williamson, S. (2004). The resilience and strengths of low-income families. *Family Relations, 53*, 159–167.

Retirement. (2011). *Heartland Monitor Poll.* Retrieved from http://heartlandmonitor.com/retirement/

Short, D. (2015, September 17). *Median household incomes by age bracket: 1967–2014.* Retrieved from http://www.advisorperspectives.com/dshort/updates/Household-Incomes-by-Age-Brackets

Strom, R. D., & Strom, P. S. (2015). Assessment of intergenerational communication and relationships. *Educational Gerontology, 41*, 41–52. doi:10.1080/03601277.2014.912454

United States Census. (2015). *Educational attainment by the population.* Retrieved from http://www.census.gov/hhes/socdemo/education/data/cps/2015/tables.html

Waldron, V., & Kelley, D. (2009). *Marriage at midlife: Analytical tools and counseling strategies.* New York, NY: Springer.

· 2 ·

CREATING THE MARRIAGES AT
MIDLIFE ARCHIVE (MaMA)

I want you, the reader of this book, to make an informed judgment about the quality of the data presented here. For that reason this chapter describes in detail the couples who participated in these interviews. I also explain the instructional context from which this project emerged and explore my own biases as an instructor, researcher, and middle-aged married person. A unique feature of this work is the involvement of students as co-researchers. In the chapter, I introduce you to some of these student interviewers and review the evidence for (and against) the quality of the interviews they conducted. For me, the insights gained by my students—what they learned about the research process and their insights about the relationships of their parents and other middle-aged couples—were nearly as important as what I learned about the resilience of midlife marriages. So, this chapter is written with the intent of being transparent about the research process and the factors that shaped my interpretations of the data.

The Marriage at Midlife Archive (MaMA) is a collection of hundreds of student-conducted interviews with romantic couples who are in the middle-stages or later stages of life. At the time of this writing, the archive includes 275 written reports produced by the interviewers and over 125 audio recordings are available to the public. The interviews range in length from roughly

20 to 60 minutes with an average of about 35 minutes, for a total of about 9600 minutes of recorded discourse (or about 160 hours). The written interview reports approximate 1200 pages of description, quoted excerpts, analysis, and reflection. The average participant is 55 years old and the couples report being in a committed relationship for at least 20 years, with a median of 28 years, and a mean of 29.6 years. Nearly all (98%) are married.

The interviews were collected by me and, more commonly my undergraduate and graduate students, all of whom were enrolled in a course I teach periodically (COM 417: Communication and Aging). The interviews were conducted as one of several options for the course's research requirement, but 96% of students choose to interview a long term romantic couple. Although the interview assignment has been in place for a decade, it was only in the last four years that I decided to view the interviews as a research project as well as a pedagogical exercise. Impressed with the authenticity and quality of many (certainly not all) of the interviews, I came to view the data as a source of relational insight that should be shared beyond the confines of my classroom. So I decided to enlist my students in an effort to build an archive of the interviews and approached my university's Internal Review Board (IRB) about this possibility. A process was created whereby both students and couples could consent to allow the data to be used for research purposes. Couples allowed the recording of the interview to be released and students permitted the use of written accounts they provided to document the interview process. Names were to be removed in any published written reports. Most couples and students (roughly 97%) gave this permission. Indeed, most couples were willing to share their experiences, even painful ones, more broadly because they hoped others could learn from their mistakes and successes. Thus the MaMA was born.

I have previously engaged many undergraduate and graduate students in the research process. And, I have directed numerous M.A. thesis projects and a handful of doctoral dissertations. But this is the first time that I have invited *all* of the students enrolled in a course to serve as co-researchers. I admit to some early reservations about this move. Could students enrolled in a senior-level undergraduate course be skilled interviewers? I should note that about 10% of students are enrolled in an enriched version of the course that counts for graduate credit. Would students take the role seriously? Or, would they simply "go through the motions," trying to meet course requirements as efficiently as possible?

As it turns out, I feel quite confident in the quality of data that remained after I culled out the few interviews that were of poor quality (less than 4%)

due to poor effort or a simple failure to follow the research protocol. In fact, I am enamored of these interviews precisely because students conducted them, often with their parents or other close social contacts. The resulting conversations are surprisingly honest and frequently quite intimate. They are sometimes awkward, particularly at first, and the couples sometimes speak in clichés ("Good communication is the key"). But typically, as the interviews progress, the students and couples become more comfortable. What are the markers of this heightened seriousness and comfort? Couples sometimes signal it explicitly with comments like, "Well, I didn't think we would go there, but you need to know that we almost divorced about eight years ago" or "I don't think we've even resolved this in our minds yet, but we just didn't agree on how to respond when your sister said she was pregnant and wanted to move home." Other times, the partners asked permission before disclosing "Is it ok if I talk about how the operation affected you?" And at still other times, the tone of the interview shifted gradually from a question-and-answer format to a free flowing conversation, with the participants offering unsolicited information, telling long and often funny stories, and even asking the interviewee questions ("Have you and your boyfriend talked about what's gonna happen if you have kids some day?").

Students often reported that they *really wanted* to know more. And, as they were encouraged to do, I hear them tactfully nudging the couple for examples and details: "When you say he became more understanding as you two grew older ... how did he *show* that to you?" Some interviews are funny and others very serious; some are halting and formal but many others are relaxed, flowing, and conversational. Although the interviews certainly vary in richness and quality, nearly all yield at least a few very concrete accounts of the changes, challenges, and opportunities that define the middle years of long relationships.

The interview reports written by the students constitute a major source of data for this book. The reporting assignment itself is detailed in Chapter 8. Students offered a synthesis and description of the interview and transcribed verbatim the answers to key questions about midlife challenges, changes, and opportunities. These were the starting point for the analysis, as the coding teams read each one, flagging potential themes. Later the recorded interviews came into play as I confirmed and elaborated on the written reports. The written reports vary in technical proficiency, as you might expect from a group of undergraduates. Some are detailed, engaging, and clear. Others are less well-developed but competent descriptions of interview content and process. A relative few are riddled with errors in spelling and grammar. Some strong interviewers turned out to be weak writers, and vice versa. But even the most-error prone written reports and the skimpiest interviews seem to turn up something concrete and interesting about these midlife couples. Excerpts from over 100 of the reports are actually cited in this book.

The Participants

During the research period, 301 interview assignments were completed but 13 of those were "alternative" assignments—typically interviews with a professional who worked intensively with aging persons. From the remaining 288 interviews, the sample was culled to 275 couples (550 individuals) after incomplete data were excluded. Cases were further excluded when data analysis revealed that couples had been together for a shorter periods of time than required for this study and if interviewers failed to follow instructions and/or excluded key interview questions. Exclusion judgments were made on a case-by-case basis because in some interviews the required questions were skipped because the information had been offered in response to earlier questions. For some analyses the sample size was 265 couples.

A large majority of the couples reported being married (98%). Marriages ranged from 20 to 45 years in length. When years in a committed relationship was the measurement criterion, the range was 20–49 years in length, with a mean of 29.6 (SD = 7.2), median of 28 years and a mode of 25 years. A few couples reported starting their committed relationship when one partner was younger than 18 years of age, but most (98%) started at age 18 or later.

At the time of the interview, the average age for husbands was 56 years (SD = 8.5). For wives it was 53.6 (SD = 8.1). The youngest participants were aged 35 at the time of the interview and 88% were below the age of 65 years. The remaining participants were in their 70s or early 80s. In each case, these participants had married later in life, often for a second time. They qualified for the study because they had been married for between 20 and 45 years. For these older couples, data analysis focused on changes, challenges, and growth during the years before they turned 65.

The majority of these relationships (67.2%) were first marriages, but more than one fifth (21.9%) were second marriages for both husband and wife. An additional 2% were third or fourth marriages. The remaining couples were mixed (e.g., first for him, second for her) or (in a few cases) unmarried in the "official" sense.

The average number of children was 2.8 (SD = 1.3) with a median of 3.0 and a mode of 2. The number of children ranged from 0 to 8. The numbers include stepchildren if they had lived with the couple or had been actively parented by them. Stepchildren who had reached adulthood prior to the marriage were not counted. Couples identified the age of their youngest child at the age of the interview. The average age of the youngest offspring was 21.6 years (SD = 7.1). Nine couples reported having a child younger than ten years old and six couples reported having offspring older than 40 years in age.

In terms of ethnicity, 53.6% of husbands and 57.7% of wives identified as white/Caucasian. The numbers for other ethnic/race categories were 11.7/9.1% (Hispanic), 6.0/4.9% (African American) 1.9/2.6% (Asian/Pacific Islander) and 0.08/1.1% (Native American). Some participants identified as having a "mixed" background, such as White/Hispanic, including 5.0% of husbands and 4.3% of wives. Roughly 13% of husbands and wives preferred to identify themselves using other labels, such as "Middle Eastern" or "Hungarian." Roughly 7% of participants chose not to provide a descriptor.

Of the participants, 36.7 were the parents or stepparents of the interviewer and 6.9% were grandparents. Another 7.2% of participants were members of the interviewer's extended family (e.g. aunts, uncles) and 6.9% were friends of the family. Another 21% we labeled "familiar contacts." This category included neighbors, parents of the interviewer's friends, and older coworkers. Other categories included parents of the interviewer's romantic partner (2.5%). Just under 19% of the sample were counted as "other/unknown." Typically these interviewees were located via referral from someone in the groups listed above. In summary, more than 80% of the interviewees were known to the interviewee and roughly 50% of them were family members.

The Course

The data were collected in the context of a course I teach at Arizona State University (Com 417: Communication and Aging). The course is a semester-long study of how communication changes across the lifespan. The students and I cover ground familiar to most of us who teach lifespan courses. For example, physiological effects of aging, such as hearing loss, on communication are considered. We also examine media stereotypes, cultural differences in the perceptions of aging, the role of media and communication technologies in the lives of older persons, and end-of-life discussions. The unique features of lifespan research are examined as well, such as cohort effects. Longitudinal survey designs also receive some attention. Here I review my approach to the course to help the reader assess how students were prepared to conduct interviews and how that preparation may have influenced the interpretative frames of references that I brought to the project.

A Focus on Aging Relationships

As I see it, COM 417 is unique in two ways. First, as I teach it, the course focuses on how *relationships* age, as well as the aging processes of individuals. The notion of relational resilience is explored. How is it that some personal relationships survive, even thrive, over long periods of time? We consider long-term sibling, parent-child, mentoring, coworker, and romantic relationships. Of these relational types, romantic relationships receive the most attention.

Why romantic relationships? The reasons are several. The students in my courses are often of traditional college age, but about 20% of them are "nontraditional students" aged 25–50 years. Both groups seem particularly interested in, and puzzled by, romantic relationships. Some have found their relationships to be short and even painful. The older group may have experienced a divorce. Or, their enrollment at the university has necessitated role adjustments in their family relationships and, in particular, their marriages. Writing for class assignments, these nontraditional students often reveal that their partners are caught off balance, stressed, and sometimes resentful of this decision. Of course many are trying to be supportive, but the disruption of relational routines is undeniable and sometimes uncomfortable.

My younger students are sometimes skeptical about marriage. A surprising number (to me) describe feeling frustrated and lost as they try to negotiate the myriad relational forms that are common to their generation. For them, the road from hooking up for sex, to friends with benefits, to semi-committed relationship is sometimes not pretty. Some are almost wistful as they describe a desire to find a steady relationship and something like "true love." But some are also relationships skeptics, having witnessed their parents' messy divorces and wary of being trapped in a relationship that might, in the long run, turn stale, deceptive, or bitter.

So it is against this backdrop that I decided to make relational resilience a connecting thread in my course. We examine the research on long marriages. In fact, one of the course texts is a book I wrote with Douglas Kelley on this topic. A translational text written for practitioners and the public, *Marriage at*

Midlife (Waldron & Kelley, 2009) documents the challenging turning points of the "middle stages" of marriage and offers strategies for working through them. The book is guided by three frameworks (role theory, resilience theories, and the lifespan approach). Doug and I have also written about the role that forgiveness can play in long term relationships (Waldron & Kelley, 2008) and I discuss some of this work in Com 417. So the students who conducted the interviews are influenced by these "sensitizing concepts."

The class discusses case studies and documentaries on the topic of long-term relationships, such as the now-classic *For Better or Worse* (Collier, 1993) which follows five couples who have been together for 50 years or more, but are also quite different on such dimensions as race/ethnicity, sexual orientation, views of sexual fidelity, and patterns of communication. Aware of cohort affects (e.g., divorce was highly stigmatized when these couples were young), our class discussions focus on what we can learn, and what we can't, from these older relationship veterans.

A Focus on Midlife

Many courses of this type are understandably focused on later life, say, the years after 65. My course certainly addresses the challenges and opportunities of life's last season. But a major focus is *midlife*, the years from roughly 40 to 64 years. This preference is grounded in a variety of my own experiences as a researcher and person who is aging. As noted in Chapter 1, middle age can be a time of changing roles, as partners with children move from active parenting to a less-child centric way of life. Certain medical conditions, such as hypertension, breast cancer, and prostate cancer appear in greater frequency. Certain changes at work, such as the assumption of significant leadership responsibilities are more common at midlife. At the same time, job loss can be more devastating as specialized and well-paid middle-aged workers are forced to seek new opportunities in an economy that may require them to learn new skills while working at a lower rate of compensation. As we observed in 2009, midlife changes such as these influence marriages and they are sometimes the cause of midlife divorce.

My students' parents are often middle-aged. And a segment of the students in my course, roughly 10%, are middle-aged or approaching it. And my own previous research on very long marriages (40 years on average; Waldron & Kelly, 2008) suggested that the middle stage of those long relationships, say 15–30 years in, can be a time of great relational adjustment—a "make or break" period. All of this is evidence for my decision to give midlife considerable attention in the course.

So my instructional biases should be coming clear. Helping students navigate their way to, and through, long and fulfilling relationships is an important goal of the course. And I think there is value in studying the trajectories of these relationships through the lifecourse, especially those middle stages of life. I ask students to play the role of co-researcher or "citizen scientist" as we investigate midlife marriages. And it is in that role that they seek a long term couple (together more than 20 years) to interview. Of course, my not-so-secret agenda is that the interview with parents, aunts and uncles, parents of friends, and other veteran couples will have some beneficial side effects for the students. I hope they will encounter ideas that will be useful in their own budding romantic relationships or in diagnosing what went wrong in those that failed. I hope that the interviews provide an "excuse" to learn more about the relationships of their parents and other older people, to initiate a meaningful intergenerational dialogue around relationships. Indeed, as we will see, students often report being surprised at the intimate disclosures, previously untold stories, and hard-won wisdom shared by these couples.

My Assumptions and Biases

Interested for many years in the practices that maintain long personal relationships, I have studied that topic in work settings, looking closely at the how supervisory and coworker relationships are maintained (e.g., Waldron, 2003; Waldron & Sanderson, 2011). Maintenance practices in families have also been a focus of my research. For example, my colleagues and I examined how long-distance bonds are maintained despite the turbulence associated with relocation and retirement (Waldron, Gitelson, & Kelley, 2005). With Douglas Kelley I have examined the role of forgiveness in repairing and redefining marriages and family relationships (Waldron & Kelly, 2008). My thinking has certainly evolved over the years and I tend now to define this stream of research using the metaphor of *resilience*, rather than *maintenance*.

Relational Resilience as a Sensitizing Concept

I first imagined the current project at a time (around 2008) when research on resilient individuals was reaching full bloom. Among the defining features of this work was an emphasis on the psychological strengths that allowed people to cope with adverse circumstances, a focus that was contrasted with the risk-based orientation of the past. Resilience is defined along various dimensions but it typically refers to a person or system's capacity to recover, or "bounce back" from adversity, disruption, or stress. Resilience can involve resisting adversity, coping, recovering, sustaining that recovery, and sometimes even growing stronger in response to difficult circumstances (Zautra, 2009). In contrast, the concept of maintenance is more limited, foregrounding the practices that sustain and stabilize a relationship, but deemphasizing responses to adversity.

I embrace this strength-based approach in my own recent work, aligning myself with other communication researchers who study positive communication. But my research questions concern resilient relationships more than resilient persons. And more than that, I am particularly interested in the *communication practices* that foster resilience in romantic relationships, marriages, and families. In this regard I am indebted to communication scholar Patrice Buzzanell (2010), who has called attention to the role of discourse in talking resilience into being. From this theoretical perspective, resilience is more than a quality that emanates from the physical, psychological, or moral character of the individual. Rather, it emerges from the discourse and material practices that enact relationships. The stories we share, the rituals we enact, the ways that we talk about adversity and strength—these provide clues to the nature of resilience.

The couples studied for this project were *not* selected because they had experienced adversity. Rather longevity was the main selection criteria. So it would be incorrect to define this project solely as a study of relational resilience. But as was the case in our previous study of much older couples (Waldron & Kelley, 2008), most partners (certainly more than 80%) interviewed for the current investigation described serious challenges and negative turning points at some time in their relationship history. In this report I focus primarily on adversity that occurred during the middle stages of life (40–65 years), and what might be defined as the "middle stage" of long relationships, roughly between the 15 and 30 year marks. So to summarize, with my students I approached the data guided in part by my interest in the communication practices that helped partners navigate potential relational challenges at midlife. And while we were interested in the nature of those challenges, we also were attuned to the potential communicative strengths exhibited by these couples.

Personal Biases: My Midlife Life

I am sure this keen interest in midlife marriages stems in part from my own experience as a middle-aged person (57 years old) in a long term relationship. Kathleen and I just celebrated our 30th wedding anniversary. During the last ten years or so we experienced many of the changes reported by the couples interviewed for this book. Our two kids left home, leaving us to deal with the role loss that many empty nesters experience. Both of our kids are in their mid-20s now and they are thriving, but they have at times experienced rocky periods of challenging mental and physical health and financial stress. We had to know how much support to give, how much to stay involved as parents.

Our parents are aging and making tough decisions about where and how to live. We grieved the loss of my father, who died after a long bout with prostate cancer. My mom and Kathleen's dad have both endured major cancer-related surgeries in the last few years. We have wondered how best to support our parents during these periods of intense illness and caregiving. When one of us has been preoccupied by worry or caregiving, the other has been there to pick up the slack in our lives. But there is no doubt that our relationships with our parents are changing and our marriage changes in response. We always relied on *them* for advice and help. And we still do. But social support now flows both ways and we know our parents will need us more as the challenges of aging and illness grow more acute.

We relocated five years ago. After raising the kids in one house for a period of 17 years, we downsized. Compared to our previous location in the suburbs, our new mid-city neighborhood seems a better fit with our "kid-less" lifestyle, with its nearby restaurants, museums, and gathering places. We met wonderful new neighbors and made new friends. But leaving our beloved family home behind was hard, particularly for Kathleen. And for a period of months, the process stressed our marriage. Indeed, as we will see in Chapter 3, relocation is a major stressor for midlife couples.

Kathleen and I have also experienced career stress and job loss. A severe economic downturn resulted in job insecurity. The university closed a program that Kathleen had worked so hard to build. For a period of several years she labored at jobs that were lower paying and less fulfilling. Even now we shudder when thinking about the emotional toll we paid during that time. And resentment at the way it all was handled still surfaces at times. As we have experienced firsthand, career-related adversity can have corrosive effects on marriages, even those that have been solid for many years.

Health is something we think about more now that we are deep into middle age. I recently experienced a health scare that required an unnerving round of tests. And we lost a dear friend to a heart attack just weeks before I wrote these sentences. And just three years ago Kathleen and I realized that we wanted different things from our summer vacations. I wanted to hike, bike, and enjoy the outdoors. Kathleen wanted to relax, read, and recharge her emotional boundaries. A ferocious argument erupted after one lengthy but unsatisfying vacation. It surfaced resentments that had built for decades. As people who study human relationships, we were surprised at the depth of our disgruntlement and the fact that we hadn't been willing to address it in the past. As you will see in the data reported in this book, midlife is a time when the emotional chickens come home to roost. After some emotional but honest arguments, we made some adjustments in our approaches to vacations and our communication practices.

So our marriage is on solid ground now, but there have been some trying moments in recent years.

All of this is to say that relational resilience has been on my personal radar. And I can see that many of my same-aged peers are experiencing similar relational stresses and adjustments. Not all long term couplings can, or should, persist. Some relationships are abusive, some are empty, and some have simply run their course. As for me, I don't want to just *be married*, to win some prize in the relationship longevity sweepstakes. I want a marriage that continues to be vital, satisfying, and loving. So far, so good. But I have to admit that, after 30 years, I still have a lot to learn about Kathleen, myself, and marriage. So sure, I conducted this study partly for selfish reasons. But I assumed that readers of this book might also be curious about marriage at midlife. I am glad to have you along for the ride.

The Student Interviewers

The contributions of student researchers are essential to the success of the MaMA project, but by asking students to join me as researchers I raised some thorny questions for myself, the students, and evaluators of this research. I want to explore those here.

Students as Co-Researchers

My students participated in key research tasks. They became familiar with an interview script, added their own supplemental questions, recruited participants, conducted interviews, created and submitted a recording of the interview, reviewed the recordings, analyzed the responses to key questions, and submitted a written synthesis and analysis of the responses, supported with verbatim quotations from the interviews. The written analysis included a reflection on the success of their interview and their own role in it. To prepare for this assignment, students read research on older persons and their relationships, became familiar with lifespan theories, and reviewed a section of the text on researching older populations (e.g. cohort effects). As advanced students most of these co-researchers had completed two research methods courses—one focused on qualitative and humanistic research methods and one on traditional quantitative/empirical approaches. All student researchers successfully completed the university-required training on research with human participants, an investment of roughly three hours. Finally, as noted in the *Acknowledgments*, a subset of students participated in later phases of data analysis, helping with such tasks as searching the transcripts for keywords, developing qualitative themes, and offering ideas during data analysis.

In contrast, most students did *not* participate in data analysis beyond that required in the class assignment (see Chapter 9). They analyzed just the single interview they conducted, using guidelines provided in the assignment. Most students did not participate in the conceptualizing or writing of this book, although I am grateful to the students who helped me puzzle through the data at an earlier stage of this project.

I should note here that I did not simply replicate the common practice of assigning undergraduates minor and routine roles in science labs or as data entry assistants. Many universities, including mine, pride themselves in engaging students in research, and often these roles benefit students and their faculty supervisors (myself included). At least in my view, the interviewing, analysis, and writing tasks my students perform are more complicated; the interview assignment is a kind of culminating experience for social science students, a chance to perform research and explore its relevance to their own relationships, and those of others they care about. As others have observed, students are not just a voice to be heard, or assistants to be delegated tasks; they can be vital members of teacher-student research partnerships (Groundwater-Smith & Mockler, 2016). Although my students make only a short term commitment to the project, I think the partnership metaphor offers a reasonable description of the contributions they make.

At a somewhat greater remove, the couples they interview enter the project in a similar spirit of collaboration. In the data I see what Way and colleagues have labelled "flickers of transformation" (Way, Zwier, & Tracy, 2015). These are discourses practices that suggest interviewer and interviewees are working together to construct and unpack their understandings of how relationships work. Examples include spontaneous probing questions offered by either party ("Oh. I am curious how that happens. How do you decide when to share your conflict with friends?"). Questions of this kind encouraged interviewees to articulate their understandings and push beyond the obvious. Other examples include identifying contradictory opinions ("I notice you two disagree on this? Can you tell me more?") and counterfactual prompting. The latter encourages the interviewee to imagine or reimagine the way things are: "If you had married earlier in life, how would things have been different?" Together these practices suggest that interviewers are moving beyond a simple question-and-answer protocol and engaging in real dialogue.

Why Choose to Engage Students as Researchers?

First, in reflecting on my own motives, I should make clear that I don't particularly need to have undergraduate students serve as co-researchers. I have collected data on the relationships of middle-aged (and older) persons for many years, and like so many researchers, have collected more data than I can possibly analyze in my remaining years! These data have been collected by me, my colleagues, and graduate research assistants, often with funding provided by external sources such as local governments, foundations, and (most recently) the National Institutes of Health. Certainly, as the project evolved, I anticipated publishing this work. My job as a research professor requires that kind of activity, so in that sense my motives were partly professional. I get paid for completing and publishing research.

Professional ambitions aside, the main reason I wanted to conceptualize students as researchers is that the interview assignments produced for my course were, on the whole, just so darn interesting! Students seemed to "take ownership" of this assignment. They worked hard to locate appropriate respondents and build rapport. Listening to the interviews I was pleased to see that they typically followed instructions meticulously. At the same time, students often improvised by adding questions spontaneously, going off-script, probing, self-disclosing, sharing humor, and voluntarily extending the interview. Students handled delicate topics, such as infidelity, with tact. They respected privacy boundaries but also probed gently for more information. The tone of the interviews was often one of respectful curiosity. Interviewees were often more forthcoming than the student expected them to be—helpful, warm, and quite willing to share relational challenges as well as triumphs. The written reports were often detailed, well supported by evidence, engaging, and often (but certainly not always!) well written.

In short, students seemed to really *care* about the assignment. It was that too-rare example of an academic task that maps clearly into the students' present lives and their plans for the relational future. Having graded hundreds of these assignments over the years, I concocted a plan, this book, to give this work a larger audience. And connected to this motive is my hope that many other students and middle-aged people will gain valuable insight from the MaMA project.

What Value Did Student Researchers Bring to the Study?

I soon learned that other social science researchers have recognized the value of undergraduates as co-researchers. Some of this reflection appears in the higher education literature, where students have been employed to research the experiences of their peers. In a representative study, undergraduates conducted focus groups and interviews with peers to explore their transition to university life (Maunder, Cunliffe, Galvin, Rogers, & Sibulele, 2013). Although students played the role of researcher, the authors observed that students were effective, in part, because "their status as fellow students enabled a particular relationship to be established with participants which, we argue, would not have been possible for a staff member to achieve" (p. 151). They argued further that the data collected by students had an authentic ring.

In our project students are certainly enacting the role of researcher, but they are also family members (sons, daughters, grandchildren, nieces or nephews), the girlfriend or boyfriend of the interviewee's offspring, a neighbor, a younger coworker, or simply an acquaintance. Rae noted that she was "interviewing my boyfriend's parents so I felt comfortable asking them outside questions aside from the one's listed that I may not have asked a couple I did not know" (#2671). Rebecca, a student in her 30s, explained:

> My husband and I look up to them and try to analyze how they do things and what has kept their relationship intact for so long and like to utilize what we have learned from them in our own marriage. (#2611)

Perhaps more than they would an anonymous researcher, interviewees seem genuinely committed to providing to these students information that is both honest and helpful. They are research participants, sure. But they often sound like concerned mentors, determined to share lessons learned though long and sometimes painful experience. As mentioned above, some of these encounters start with the slightly clunky sound of a formal research interview, but they often evolve to comfortable conversations. As in the peer-to-peer interviews reported by Maunder and colleagues, the data collected by students has an "authentic ring" largely because student and interviewer seem genuinely committed to understanding the dynamics of long relationships.

Quality of the Data

In assessing the data, I am influenced by the work of scholars who have written extensively about criteria for assessing qualitative work. For example, Tracy (2010) described eight "big tent" criteria that prove useful in assessing studies across the various genres of qualitative inquiry. Among those that increase my confidence in the data are topic worthiness, sincerity, resonance, and ethics. The worthiness of the topic comes in part from the surge of interest in the research literature in the topic of relational resilience, particularly at mid-life. But more compelling is importance that *interviewees* find in the topic, as evidenced by their willingness to invest up to an hour in the interview and their frequent comments about the significance of the long-term relationship in their lives. When asked toward the beginning of the interview about how attitudes have changed toward marriage, respondents offered comments about the importance of their marriages and the difficulty of maintaining them. In their verbal and nonverbal behaviors they conveyed a sense of engagement, seriousness, and interest. Indeed, sharing fully their relational experiences, as one spouse called it, "the good, bad, and ugly," with these (mostly) young interviewers was to them a worthy goal.

Tracy (2010) argues that the sincerity of a project is evident in its transparency and self-reflexivity. Students have agreed to make their interview reports publically available in the archive and many of the oral recordings are also available for review. A requirement of the interview assignment is that students reflect honestly on their performance as an interviewer. Their reports often describe that which went well, as was the case with Carlos who said "the couple was very comfortable and talkative and gave answers that they took a second to think about. They meant what they said and were able to be honest with me" (#269i). The recording confirms that the conversation was relaxed and warm. But many students, including Wei Ling, were unflinching in identifying difficulties.

> One of the things that I think I could still get better at is the overall flow of the interviewing process. I feel like at times I can make it more conversational and more just asking questions. Another thing that I think that I can improve on is being able to come up with follow-up questions on the fly based off what the person has told me.

As Tracy (2010) describes it, resonance is the capacity of the data to move the reader. The findings should appear applicable to the lives of others, including the reader. Although this judgment must be made by you, I find indirect evidence in the written reflections of the interviewers. They often write about how the interview assignment helps them improve their own relationships. Some better understand their own parents after interviewing a couple of the same age and circumstances. Along with my team of coders, most of whom were middle-aged married women, I found myself frequently identifying with many of the couples. The interview data sparked deep and sometimes emotional conversation among us, often accompanied by disclosure about the trials and tribulation of our own marriages. All of this is to say, the data ring true.

With regard to ethics, my quality claims rest on several foundations. Of course, all student interviewers and interviewees gave informed consent, or their data are not reported here. As promised, names were changed in this report. In the reporting of these results I take considerable care to do no harm, changing details of incidents (e.g. infidelity) that might cause severe distress to people beyond the study sample. Couples who might be distressed by the interview were encouraged to contact me so they might be referred to support services. I detected no signs of serious distress in the interviews and no one contacted me. In fact, many couples seemed to enjoy the process and for some, it seemed to reignite conversations about their commitment and how it might be sustained in the future. Students were encouraged to share their interview reports (and the recording) with the couple. In that way, the couple might learn from the literature cited by the student and from the students' often astute observations.

Authorship ethics was another consideration. If students are co-researchers, should they be coauthors? The publication manual of the American Psychological Association (2010) provides some guidance on this issue, suggesting that authorship is conveyed to those who make "substantial scientific contributions" (p. 18). The single interview completed by undergraduates does not meet that standard. Students who engaged in the early rounds of data analysis made a more substantial contribution of their time and talent. They were recognized as coauthors of a conference paper and Chapter 3. Since that time, approximately 250 additional interviews have been analyzed and the project has evolved considerably. So I chose to recognize a host of students in the Acknowledgments section, but felt authorship was justified for only a few.

For Tracy (2010) and many other qualitative analysts (e.g., Corbin & Strauss, 2008; Creswell, 2007; Ellingson, 2008) perhaps the overriding quality concern is the extent to which the researcher's claims are credible. Credibility is derived from detailed data and thick description; it avoids oversimplification. As Ellingson has suggested in her discussion of crystalization, qualitative researchers often draw upon multiple perspectives, methods, and types of data to construct a layered, nuanced understanding. As I survey the work reported here I can construct arguments supporting and rejecting the credibility of the research. A portion of the student interviews seem stilted and (as Wei Ling notes above) the interviewers sometimes miss opportunities to probe for details. Additional interview practice might have yielded richer data in these cases. Another concern: the audio recordings reveal that couples vary considerably in the verbal dexterity with which they describe their relationships. Some offer only brief observations ("We just love each other") and platitudes ("Marriage is hard work"). It is hard to know if these brief offerings are meaningful to the couple or if they are offered merely to help the interviewer complete the assignment.

Yet when I look across the 275 interviews and more than 1200 pages of interview reports, the larger corpus of data appears rich, deep, and reflective of the great variety found in romantic relationships. Moreover, the credibility of the data is enhanced by the dyadic nature of the interviews, as partners give voice to both diverging and similar views of their relationship. Perhaps 15% of the interviews are dominated by wife or husband, but for the most part, both partners contribute substantially; both add at least a few unique observations. In this way, the multi-vocal nature of the relationships is preserved in our data. The process itself, and the interview questions, have evolved over the course of this project. Prior to the collection of the current interviews, I fine-tuned the questions to redress shortcomings discovered in earlier iterations. For example, a question about "the last ten years" was added to prompt the couple to consider the more recent past, not the early stages of the relationship. For the average couple (married nearly 30 years and roughly 55 years of age) that instruction focuses attention on the period between 20 and 30 years of marriage and ages 45–55. Another quality improvement was the designated series of questions that every student interviewer must ask, using the very same wording (see Chapter 9). In that way, I am assured that every couple is asked the same questions, although interviewers are strongly encouraged to ask spontaneous follow-up questions, to invent their own inquiries, and to adopt a conversational style as the interview progresses.

In the end, the credibility of this report will be determined in large part by the quality of the data reported in Chapters 4–7. But I think the evidence is largely favorable. The student-led interviews often have a feel of authenticity. The data are extensive and often nuanced. This report juxtaposes multiple points of view: student, romantic partners, mine, and those of various coding teams who have worked with me to define and refine the themes reported in later chapters. It certainly is not true that the "data speaks for itself." Instead it is filtered through the assumptions, processes, and biases detailed in this chapter. Nonetheless, my hope it that the voices featured in this book resonate with you.

References

Buzzanell, P. M. (2010). Presidential address—Resilience: Talking, resisting, and imagining, new normalcies into being. *Journal of Communication, 60*, 1–14.

Collier, D. (Producer). (1991). *For better or for worse* [DVD]. Available from http://www.studiobfilms.com/for-better-for-worse/

Corbin, J., & Strauss, A. (2008). *Basics of qualitative research*. Thousand Oaks, CA: Sage.

Creswell, J. W. (2007). *Qualitative inquiry and research design: Choosing among five approaches*. Thousand Oaks, CA: Sage.

Ellingson, L. L. (2008). *Engaging crystallization in qualitative research*. Thousand Oaks, CA: Sage.

Groundwater-Smith, S., & Mockler, N. (2016). From data source to co-researchers? Tracing the shift from "student voice" to student-teacher partnerships in educational action research. *Educational Action Research, 24*, 159–176.

Maunder, R. E., Cunliffe, M., Galvin, J., Rogers, J., & Sibulele, M. (2013). Listening to student voices: Student researchers exploring undergraduate experiences of university transition. *Higher Education, 66*, 139–152. doi:10.1007/s10734-012-9595-3

Tracy, S. J. (2010). Qualitative quality: Eight "big-tent" criteria for excellent qualitative research. *Qualitative Inquiry, 16*, 837–851.

Waldron, V. (2003). Relationship maintenance in organizational settings. In D. Canary & M. Dainton (Eds.), *Maintaining relationships through communication: Relational, contextual, and cultural variations* (pp. 163–184). New York, NY: Lawrence Erlbaum.

Waldron, V., Gitelson, R., & Kelley, D. (2005). Gender differences in social adaptation to a retirement community: Longitudinal changes and the role of mediated communication. *Journal of Applied Gerontology, 24,* 283–298.

Waldron, V., & Kelley, D. (2008). *Communicating forgiveness.* Newbury Park, CA: Sage.

Waldron, V., & Kelley, D. (2009). *Marriage at midlife: Analytical tools and counseling strategies.* New York, NY: Springer.

Waldron, V., & Sanderson, J. (2011). The role of subjective threat in upward influence attempts. *Communication Quarterly, 59,* 239–254.

Way, A. K., Zwier, R. K., & Tracy, S. J. (2015). Dialogic interviewing and flickers of transformation: An examination and delineation of interactional strategies that promote participant self-reflexivity. *Qualitative Inquiry, 12,* 720–731. doi:10.1177/1077800414566686

Zautra, A. J. (2009). Resilience: One part recovery, two parts sustainability. *Journal of Personality, 77*(6), 1935–1943.

SECTION II

WHAT THE COUPLES SAY

· 3 ·

MIDLIFE CHANGES AND CHALLENGES

Amy Przytula Vynalek, Catalina Cayetano,
Dayna N. Kloeber, and Amanda Tuholsky

This chapter explores the challenging events and lifecourse changes that couples report experiencing during the middle stages of long marriages. Just to be clear, the purpose of this chapter is not to paint a gloomy picture. In Chapter 1, I presented data showing that middle-age can be a time of stability and wellbeing. But we also saw that this period of life is often punctuated by major changes and strained by grinding stressors. In this chapter I present both quantitative and qualitative data describing the number and types of adversity reported by our couples. What emerges is a picture of midlife as a period rich in relational challenge and change, one that sometimes calls for reassessment and reinvention. For some couples, this is a period of adversity due to *involuntary* changes such as job loss or the onset of illness. For others, *voluntary changes*, such as a decision to change careers or return to school, were the source of relational adversity. As these couples navigated this part of the lifecourse some encountered watershed moments—turning points that prompted substantial and rapid change. For others, midlife was a time when the grind of chronic stressors left the relationship brittle and vulnerable. The good news is that the couples we spoke with had thus far weathered this period; faced with adversity they stuck together and some forged more resilient bonds. Many were pleased with the way their relationship had changed, others were disappointed, and still others were working out the details of an evolving relational identity.

The data reported in this chapter were produced using the methods reported in Chapter 8, including qualitative thematic analysis, keyword searching, and metaphor analysis. In the first section I report the results of an analysis of challenges and stressors couples reported experiencing at midlife (For an early version, see Waldron, Przytula Vynalek, Kloeber, Cayentano, & Froke, 2014). The second section explores the metaphors they used to describe this period of this phase of their long relationships.

The coding process yielded 13 categories of midlife challenges or stressors. Table 3.1 includes brief descriptions of each challenge, including the synonymous terms that were used for keyword searching. The number of couples (out of 265) reporting each kind of challenge is indicated as both a frequency and a percentage. These numbers are not cumulative because couples often

Table 3.1. Relational challenges at midlife.

Relational challenge	Descriptive terms	Frequency (%)
Distinctive Challenges		
Illness	Sickness, health problems, cancer	86 (32.4)
Relocation	Moving (the household)	69 (26.0)
Empty nest	Offspring leave home; move out	62 (23.3)
Death of family member	Close contacts die; pass away	56 (21.1)
Financial hardship	Job loss, bankruptcy, financial stress	49 (18.4)
Boomerang kids	Offspring return; moving home	41 (15.4)
Physical intimacy	Sex, "relations"	28 (10.5)
Mental health	Depression, anxiety, panic attacks	22 (8.3)
Addiction	Alcoholism, drinking, drug abuse	17 (6.4)
Infidelity	Affair, cheating, betrayed, adultery	9 (3.4)
Custodial grandparents	Grandchildren living in home	8 (3.0)
Intersecting Challenges		
Difficult adult offspring	Addictions, job loss, legal troubles, etc.	N/A
Relational stressors	Aggression, drift, rigidity, grievances	N/A

Note: N = 265 couples; Descriptive terms were sued in key word searches of the database.

reported multiple challenges. If a change had occurred before or after midlife as we defined it (ages 40–65; length of committed relationships 15–35 years) it was excluded from this analysis. A few exceptions were allowed because the classification criteria sometimes conflicted. For example, one female partner was 35 years old but had been married for 18 years.

This coding exercise convinced us that most of the categories listed in the table represented a *distinct* challenge. During discussions about whether or not categories should be collapsed, we erred on the side of preserving the diversity of these couples' experiences. As a case in point, mental and physical health challenges could have been grouped under the single umbrella category of health, but the relational consequences of these types of adversity were sometimes quite different. As just one example, a spouse reported that his wife's reluctance to seek help for depression (due to family stigma) was a source of relational adversity. Although other pairs cited the failure to seek treatment for a *physical* ailment as a midlife challenge, depression was a unique source of adversity in midlife relationships. In another example, a female partner felt isolated because her spouse asked her not to talk with family or friends about his diagnosis.

In addition to these distinct challenges, several of the themes that emerged during qualitative coding proved difficult to quantify because they overlapped with others or were expressed in such varied forms. These *intersecting challenges* are addressed separately in this chapter and in Table 3.1.

Distinct Midlife Challenges

Eleven distinct midlife challenges/stressors are discussed in this section.

Physical Health: "He saw life through a different perspective"

Physical health was the most frequent midlife relational challenge mentioned in our interviews. Relationships were tested by battles with such diseases as prostate or breast cancer, heart attacks, and injuries due to accidents. Chronic conditions also stressed these couples, including diabetes, heart disease, and fibromyalgia. In addition to the obvious suffering of the afflicted person, these health challenges stressed relationships. Several stressors are evident in this excerpt from a lightly edited report submitted by Regina, who interviewed Nancy and Andy, a couple who had been married for 40 years.

In 2003, Andy was diagnosed with stage three melanoma which resulted in scheduling surgery very quickly and receiving statistics that frightened Andy, Nancy, and their children and grandchildren. Nancy experienced fear and a certain "gratefulness" to her husband because the thought of his having to battle cancer "revived her love" in a sense. Nancy felt that in the years prior to this, she had not been paying enough attention to her husband and experienced a struggle with communicating her affection. She quickly readjusted ... as she cared for him after his surgery and also while he underwent radiation treatment. ... Andy experienced a significant amount of depression as he was recovering from surgery and also undergoing radiation treatments. While he appreciated Nancy's help, he also "saw life through a different perspective" after being diagnosed and became angry at Nancy for her lack of "presence" in their marriage during the years prior to his diagnosis. While Nancy was working extra hours at work to make ends meet, caring for Andy while he was sick, and doing her best to recover their marriage, Andy was ... struggling to forgive past transgressions and feelings. [#177i]

Serious illness stimulated several couples to consider a "different perspective" and develop a heightened appreciation for the relationship. But as in this case, health problems also led to depression, caretaker fatigue, and mixed emotions. Our couples described feeling fear for the future of the relationship but also resentment (and subsequent guilt) toward the ill partner, especially when the illness was a result of unhealthy lifestyle choices. Allison interviewed her Uncle Roger and Aunt Janet about the effects of his heart problems on their relationship. It turned out that for many years they had saved for the "trip of a lifetime," a three-week tour of Scotland. They were forced to cancel the trip, a fact that left her "devastated" and "holding a grudge" [#281w].

As this example suggests, the health challenges of midlife can disrupt relational routines and plans, dash expectations, and call forth deep and sometimes unexpected emotions.

Relocation: *"My husband made a huge sacrifice for my career"*

In previous work, I have been surprised to see that relocation can be a highly disruptive event for midlife couples. With my former student and current colleague Dayna Kloeber, I wrote a chapter exploring the reasons (Waldron & Kloeber, 2009). Among them are differences in spousal preferences for change and stability, the difficulty of embedding in the new community, unrealistic or unmet expectations regarding the advantages of the move, disrupted family and friendship networks, one spouse feeling "forced" to move, and career complications for one or both spouses. Within our sample, relocation was a prominent midlife stressor, with more than a quarter of couples mentioning it.

Even for veteran couples relocation could be problematic, sometimes due to *differences in expectation*. Pete and Carolyn have been married 37 years. After retirement, they relocated to Arizona from the Midwest. Pete was looking forward to warm winters without snow and he convinced his wife that moving closer to family would enrich their lives. They were interviewed by a family friend, who reported the following:

> Not too long after their relocation to the Phoenix area the move began to have a negative effect on their day-to-day lives, as well as their relationship as a whole. Carolyn struggled with the move in a much more severe way than Pete did. She soon became very depressed with her new place to live and also became a lot more difficult to get along with, describing herself as a person who was "better off being left alone than interacting with other people." Pete kept himself busy during this time period by doing activities such as volunteering at the local food bank. As time wore on, the relocation never seemed to get easier for Carolyn, which ultimately has led them to go back home to Indiana. [#143i]

As Carolyn explained, she had "lived her whole life" in one community and she couldn't "cut the emotional ties" that bound her to that place and its people.

For some younger couples, midlife relocation was a *balancing act* between the needs of the partners. Consider Tina and Butch, who have been married for 23 years and still have several children living at home. To advance Tina's career, they recently relocated to China.

> My husband made a huge sacrifice when he retired early from a career he really enjoyed. We were going to a new, unknown country and had no idea what kind of experiences would face us; but we were committed to what we thought would be good for my career and for our childrens' growth and development.

Although many couples find relocation to be energizing and enriching, this theme of sacrifice was echoed in a significant portion of the interviews. Relocation was often described as a struggle or a major challenge by one or both partners. After she graduated from college, Randi's parents quit their jobs, sold the house, and moved closer to her. Unfortunately, it took nearly a year for her mother to find a job and the couple experienced a "huge struggle" both emotionally and financially. As do many midlife couples, Randi's parents eventually found decent jobs and reestablished what they considered to be "normal life."

The Empty Nest: *"We didn't prepare for the dismemberment of our family"*

The third most frequently-mentioned midlife challenge was children moving out of the family home, leaving parents with the proverbial "empty nest."

More than 20% of the couples described this as a source of stress. The empty nest is an unnecessarily limiting metaphor (Mount & Moas, 2015). Among other inadequacies it fails to recognize that adult offspring often cycle in and out of the home, parenting continues even as offspring live elsewhere, and the lives of most parents are quite full and satisfying after the children depart. Indeed, the majority of interviewees either welcomed their kids leaving home or simply didn't mention it, a finding consistent with research indicating that couples react in a variety of ways (Bouchard, 2014). And, of course, partners who never had children are unlikely to view their home as an empty nest. Nonetheless, interviewees frequently use this term and the metaphor does appear to resonate with many couples (Waldron & Kelly, 2009).

A recurrent theme in these accounts was the feeling of *identity loss*. These mothers and fathers were highly identified with their parenting job, finding meaning in their roles as guides, protectors, and nurturers. During the interview with her parents, Kara's mother reminded her that "she used to text me every night to make sure I was alive" [#158i]. Amanda interviewed her parents, describing them this way.

> They have spent almost their entire marriage focused on their two children. They are the parents that never missed a basketball game, dance recital, or family trip. Now they have to *plan* trips to visit each of their children and adjust to not having their entire family together for every holiday or event. This has been a hard transition for them because they really do value their family above anything else. [#192i]

Finding that their adult children no longer needed this level of parental investment, some parents lost their way. Sandra's mother, Sophia, reported being "so lost" when her youngest daughter left home. Sandra described her as "confused" and "in crisis" [#106i]. Married to Sophia for 23 years, Santos has noticed changes in their marriage: they have nothing to talk about. Sandra translates for us:

> Because their main relational focus has always been their kids, Santos disclosed that the kids' lives are what they always communicated about. Some examples he gave were involving sports, grades, and behavior. These topics have always consumed their dialogue. Now, he claims, he does not really know how to talk about anything else, so they are struggling. [#106i,h]

In some cases, one parent appeared to grieve more than the other. It was more often mothers who described these feelings. But fathers often articulated feelings of loss or discombobulation. The adversity attributed to the empty nest was characterized as a relational challenge, not just an emotional reaction of individual partners. Enrique is a self-employed painter who immigrated from Mexico with Maria, his wife of 36 years. Maria stayed at home to raise their three daughters and one son, all now young adults. His use of the term *dismemberment* is jarring.

> All our children started leaving little by little. We started feeling a change. A lot of times that caused frustrations between us. We started fighting because we felt that something was falling out of our hands and we didn't know how to detain it. We didn't mentally prepare ourselves for the dismemberment of our family. It caught us by surprise. (#208h)

As their interviewer and son Roberto wrote, the couple not only clashed, they actually "competed" for the affections of their children. Indeed, differential relationships with adult offspring have been previously identified as a source of midlife duress (Henry & Miller, 2004).

The importance of departing offspring in the lives of these couples was often communicated via emotion words, such as "sadness," "heartbroken," "fear," or "worry." But the feelings were sometimes mixed, as was revealed in an interview with Ron and Jill, who have been married for 26 years and raised three children into adulthood. Hallie, their interviewer (and middle child), reported:

> The couple laughed to one another and disclosed that they felt like throwing a party when their oldest daughter Amanda moved out. They admitted, though, that when their son Robbie moved out, Jill was "bawling for two days." When I asked what brought forth those emotions, Jill explained that it's "a combination of excitement and sadness." As a parent, they felt successful for raising children who can now support themselves. It was nice to see them leave because there are no more messes and late nights. On the other hand, the quiet in the house reminds them that they no longer can have those goofy moments together and it's hard not to miss them being around. [174i]

As we will learn in later chapters, many couples interpret the departure of their children as a time of excitement, joy, pride, and hard-won freedom. Even as they stay engaged with offspring, these parents describe the midlife period as a time for personal and relational growth. But as the comments above suggest, for many middle-aged couples, the emptying of the nest is a time of disruption, adversity, and confusion.

Death of a Family Member: *"Our greatest challenge as a couple, but it brought us together"*

For many people death becomes a reality only at midlife. More than in the early years of marriage, couples experience the death of friends, coworkers and valued members of the extended family. Sadly, some of our couples lost their adult offspring. Parents fell ill and passed away. The death of a parent certainly took an emotional toll on the grieving son or daughter, but couples described relational adversity as well. For Alice and Jeff, this was evidenced in reallocation of relational resources. Within a short period of time Jeff lost both of his parents and Alice lost her mother. When Jeff's dad died, the couple committed to spending more time with his grieving mother. Then Alice's mother became terminally ill. "There was no question I would take care of her. I was the oldest of my siblings and there was no other option" [#173w]. She described this period as deeply taxing for her and the marriage.

The loss of a child sometimes frayed relationships. Will and Rachel recently lost their adult son to cancer. They live in California where they were interviewed by their granddaughter.

> They told me that this tragedy put a great strain on their relationship. It had been especially hard on my grandmother who spent a very long time grieving. Even during this interview, you could tell that this subject was hard for her to talk about. She told me that after their son's death, they didn't really interact much with each other. They instead, "skated past each other" and went about with their day-to-day activities. [#273i]

Most couples endured and eventually found reason to be optimistic once again. The untimely death of their son was "… our greatest challenge as a couple, but it brought us closer together," Mike confessed [#176]. Life has yet to return to normal, and it may never do so. But Mike and his wife Meg comfort and support one another.

Financial Hardship: *"I can't retire now, because of him"*

Nearly a fifth of our couples (18.4%) described financial hardships during the middle years of their marriages. The prominence of this stressor is consistent with earlier studies (Henry & Miller, 2004). A frequent stressor was the loss of a job. But couples also described lost family businesses, bankruptcy, and failed investments. Some of the older couples were stressed by insufficient retirement income. The problems were often accompanied by descriptions of financial belt-tightening, teamwork, and role adjustments. "Tightening the belt" was a metaphor that emerged in a previous study of the language used by parents as they fostered family resilience in the face of financial hardship (Lucas &

Buzzanell, 2012). In the current study, role adjustment most often took the form of the unemployed partner accepting additional domestic duties while the working partner worked longer hours or located a higher paying position. Married 29 years, Art and Tessa described this experience to their son.

> The largest adjustment that they have encountered was Art losing his job due to the drop in the economy. Thankfully they both work, so Tessa's job was able to provide for their needs during that period of time, however … Art felt that his frustration and disappointment toward his unemployment impeded his communication with Tessa. She also was confused with their new roles and was hesitant to talk with him about her feelings, so their communication faltered until they reached their breaking points and were forced to talk out their problems. They found that Art's role loss as a provider left him in a sort of limbo until they got their communication back on track and he gained more of a housekeeping role while he searched for jobs. Tessa was relieved of stress when Art took her housekeeping role and left her as the main provider. [#008i]

As in this case, *role loss* and the need to change relational routines contributed to the financial stress created by the loss of a job.

Another theme in the interviews involved *blame*. At midlife, some couples report unresolved feelings of blame and bitterness (Waldron & Kelly, 2009). Resolving long-lasting disputes may be a key to relational resilience at this point in the lifespan. In the current study, partners sometimes blamed themselves or the other partner for bad financial decisions. "I can't retire now, because of *him*," an obviously bitter Leslie reported [#101w]. Her husband Morris apparently made some bad investments and, in her mind, hasn't worked hard enough to recover the lost income. In another example, Angel decided to go into the custom furniture business, but his gambit stressed the family's finances. There were "constant arguments" about money, his wife Yessica recalls [#132w]. She had just returned to school and the tuition bills were another source of strain. After 20 years of marriage, the couple actually divorced, largely due to financial stress. However, the silver lining to this otherwise dark situation was that both partners became more mature managers of money. Now, several years later they are happily remarried to each other. Even at midlife, couples struggled to communicate about their finances. Indeed, in providing advice to student interviewers, perhaps the most common suggestion made by couples was to "get on the same page" about money.

Boomerang Children: *"It was time for him to have a job and pay rent"*

Roughly 15% of our couples described challenges with "boomerang kids," adult children who had left the family home for a period of time, but then returned. Children who left home for advanced schooling are not counted here, as they often are expected to return for short periods of time (Bouchard, 2014). Instead, this category concerns adult children who were expecting the move to be permanent. In most cases, so were the parents. But it was certainly the case that some couples were unsurprised when their offspring moved back home. As I note below, many parents seemed to welcome the return and it was quite common for families to successfully negotiate this transition. However, to be included in this section, the boomerang had to be viewed as a source of adversity.

One source of stress was partners' *conflicting expectations*. One partner welcomes the return of the child while the other is more reluctant. One wants to impose time limits on the stay and specify rules of conduct (e.g., the returnee should help with certain domestic tasks) but the other prefers a more open-ended approach. The differences created relational tensions and sometimes erupted in destructive conflict. Elaine and Rick have been married for 30 years. They were interviewed by a friend of their daughter who knew them well. She summarized the situation with their son James.

> When James graduated college he decided to move back in for financial reasons ... Elaine thought, as his mother, he should have been able to come back without paying a dime for rent. And Rick disagreed. He said "it was time for him to have a job and pay rent. I was nervous he would get comfortable in his situation moving back home." As Elaine explained, "James saw the tension and he pulled his act together." ... While Elaine wanted to help her son, Rick wanted him to take responsibility for his actions. [#216i,h,w]

As this example suggests, a number of these couples described significant ambivalence over this midlife dilemma. How could they be supportive and nurturing while simultaneously nudging their young adult toward maturity and independence?

In some cases, *parent-offspring tensions* are problematic. By extension the marital relationship is tested. Malcolm has observed this dynamic between his father and his 21-year-old younger brother. "My dad and my brother find it extremely hard to negotiate their boundaries, arguments constantly arise ... my dad finds it hard to see my brother's point of view and vice versa. This leaves my mom to be the mediator" [#88I]. Another couple, Will and Jen, have raised four sons but now two of them have boomeranged. Will reported that this development has caused "upheaval" in their lives and reports friction in the relationship with his sons. In contrast, Jen reported feeling a "void" after the kids left. Her husband has found a second career as a youth coach and she feels disappointment at being excluded from this consuming new activity. The return of her sons seems to have, at least temporarily, renewed her sense of purpose.

Other couples interpreted the returning of their children as a *relational infringement*. A common theme in these interviews is appreciation of the freedom they experience once the kids leave home. Such constraints as meal planning, coordinating work schedules, and catering to kids' preferences for entertainment are relaxed. Numerous couples described improved sexual freedom and a relaxed intimacy. "Yikes!" Laura wrote when reporting this comment by her father: "We're finding ways to live in a big, empty house without you guys—at least we can run around naked now" [#108h]. For some parents, including Laura's dad, the return of their offspring curtailed some newly-appreciated freedoms.

Finally, couples described *financial burdens*. Parents expressed concern about the financial prospects of their children and this sometimes was the rationale for harboring boomeranged offspring. Their idea was to help the kids save money or recover from financial failure. But in their generosity some parents sacrificed their own financial well-being. The case of Tricia and Ray, as reported by family friend Kelly, is one of the more extreme examples. But their challenge is familiar to a number of our couples.

> Their "stay at home" kids consist of their son Ray who is disabled and needs assistance for several tasks that the average person can do on their own. Ray is currently unemployed and is in the process of looking for a job. Jerrod is 21, works at a convenience store, and moved his pregnant girlfriend in the house ... lastly their 24 your old daughter Candice, who currently moved back in after being out of state for college. The couple found themselves taking money out of their savings to help ends meet and prepare for their first grandchild. ... The couple do agree that their children wouldn't "survive" out in the real world right now because it's expensive to live out on your own. They came up with a plan for each of their children to save up money for future rent, pay off bills and become financially stable so they don't fall flat on their face with debt. [#124i]

Physical Intimacy: *"We have become friends, and that's just it. That's the problem"*

About 10% of our couples discussed midlife changes in sexuality. Midlife has been previously identified as a time of when sexual relationships are "shook up" (Lodge & Umberson, 2012). For some the issue was learning to reconnect sexually after a long period of intensive parenting (see "empty nest") above. In contrast, May and Ernesto found that their busy work schedules left them "too tired" for sex [#196]. After the kids left home these two immersed themselves in their careers. "Twelve to sixteen hour days were not uncommon for us; actually they were normal," Ernesto noted and Mae was spending half of her work days traveling outside the U.S. The pair realized they needed to cut back on work if they were to rekindle their romance. In contrast, Samantha and Forest realized that intimacy may not be a crucial part of their midlife relationship. "It definitely helps if you marry your best friend," Samantha explained. She characterizes their relationship as a life-long friendship and she speaks favorably about their improving communication. But the relationship lacks intimacy, in part a result of an affair that Forest initiated years ago. "We have become friends, and that's just it. That's the problem" [#286].

Health challenges affected sexual intimacy. Morris says he thinks sex was "good before I got sick" but a mild stroke makes it hard for him "to get my true feelings out" [#101]. The partners have drifted apart in recent years and spend little time together. During an intimate interview with her mother, Carrie learned that her parents' "intimacy had gone down" because her mother's kidney disease left her too tired for sex [#100].

Several couples saw midlife as a time to repair intimacy problems that had developed over the years. Janelle loved being a mom to her two kids, but she realized now that she viewed herself as "only a mother." She felt unattractive and "frumpy." Her sex life with husband Brad waned, not for physical reasons, she claims, but because they lacked emotional closeness. He admitted that sex was a root cause of many conflicts and confessed that he had devalued Janelle's contributions as a stay-at-home mom. Now, years later, Janelle has "redefined herself" by returning to school and obtaining a satisfying job. The partners better understand the sources of their cooled ardor and are tentatively growing closer [#130w].

Mental Health: *"Your father would become really depressed about having lost his job"*

Challenges were included in this category if one or both partners identified depression, anxiety, or other psychiatric conditions as a primary source of distress. These concerns were often linked to other midlife stressors, such as illness, addiction, or death of a family member, as Deisy discovered when she interviewed her best friend's parents, Perla and Jesus.

> When I asked her what made her depressed, she kind of got embarrassed and didn't want to say ... so Jesus asked Perla if it was ok for him to tell me why she was depressed

and she was ok with that. What ended up happening was after Jesus had his two major heart attacks his doctor advised him to not have sex until he recovered from the heart attack and for his blood pressure to go down. (interview notes, p. 27)

So Perla's depression was related to a lack of physical intimacy. She seemed comfortable talking about this mental health challenge, but not its cause, perhaps due to social stigma. The fact that Jesus could put the cause into words suggests that the partners are working collaboratively to manage this challenge.

Depression was sometimes a reaction to illness, injury, or job loss, or some combination of those factors. Some midlife couples were caught off guard, having never expected to deal with these kinds of events nor the depression that followed. Michael related his father's experience:

From the time he initially got hurt to when he had to retire was a period of five years. During that timeframe they did face issues they had never dealt with. There were some depression issues and fear of "now what?" My dad was dealing with leaving a career he enjoyed and working through various treatments/surgeries for his back. Now that he is two years out from his final surgery and retirement, they have discovered their relationship is back to "normal." [#025i]

Darcy's parents told a similar story, with depression arising from her father's job loss and the couple's worries about the future of their family. In this case, the effects appear to be lingering as evidenced by her father's frustration.

They only had my mother's teaching salary to live off of, which was difficult for them. I was ... thinking about college, so they also shared the stress of how this change was going to affect me. "Your father would become really depressed about having lost his job," my mother explained. My father still seemed frustrated with the situation, though he has been with his new job for a few years now. [12i]

Addiction: *"Their relationship was on the line if Frank did not stop drinking"*

Seventeen couples described challenges related to alcohol and drug abuse. Frank lost his job, in part due to excessive drinking. He and Cathy agreed that this was a time of great distress because they had to rely on Cathy's work as a part-time bookkeeper. "I am a skilled worker," Frank said. "I do well in interviews, but I have had some mishaps having to do with my alcoholism and I think that is a factor in why I am not getting called back after my third interview. It is a small industry that I am in" [#113h]. Frank is working again and staying sober. But Cathy noted that "their relationship was on the line if Frank did not stop drinking."

Indeed, alcoholism nearly broke several of these marriages. The addicted partner's willingness to seek treatment often made the difference because it left the spouse feeling more confident that currently difficult circumstances would improve in the future. But, as we learned from Amy and Chris, improvement typically came after the sober partner refused to be an enabler. Within the last ten years Chris' addiction threatened the couple's relationship. Amy reported that she had to give Chris "an ultimatum." In fact, she moved out of the house and the couple separated for several months. This event motivated Chris to enter a rehabilitation facility and he has been sober for six years. Happy and stable now, the couple shared their story in the spirit of a cautionary tale. [045w,h]

Infidelity: *"She felt so betrayed that she started to have anxiety attacks"*

Although infidelity can occur at any time in the lifecourse of a relationship, cheating at midlife was associated with unique challenges. These couples had invested in their relationships for many years and they describe the relational costs as heavy. With a track record of longevity, partners were sometimes "caught by surprise" by sexual infidelity. In their accounts one hears evidence of a world view that has shaken to its foundations. Deep uncertainty and confusion were expressed, along with such feelings as guilt, hurt, anxiety, injustice, wariness, and bitterness. In light of these disruptive effects, reconstruction of the relationship was challenging, to say the least. The nine couples who described affairs remained together at the time of our interview, but all were still repairing the damage.

> Lei stated that, at one point she thought Fei was cheating on her with his ex-girlfriend and she felt so betrayed that she started to have anxiety attacks and that took a toll on their relationship. It took a long time for her to get over [it] by visiting psychiatrists and family counseling. ... [#036]

The issue remains contentious, and Fei contends that he "did not cheat on her and that she was over-reacting to him having lunch with a friend." The partners became quiet for a while, so the interviewer moved to the next question. But later, Lei revealed that the affair had long term effects: "I just felt our relationship was not the same."

Deon and Sharonda are in their late 40s. She holds a job in the financial industry and he is a technician. In a surprisingly candid (and sometimes uncomfortable) interview conducted by a family friend, they revealed that a chronic challenge had been:

... Deon's infidelity and closedness regarding his infidelity. Sharonda's facial expression further confirmed that Deon's infidelity has truly been the biggest marital challenge for her. She struggled and continues to struggle with forgiving his past transgressions. However, after being separated from one another for a little while she was better equipped to accept the things she could not change and learned to actually deal with the hurt she experienced. After the separation, the couple renewed their relationship commitment and negotiated changing expectations. While it is evident that her biggest defeats in life are her husband's actions, Deon also mentioned how he struggled with his own demons of trying to commit to his wife and marriage. [#105i]

As a group, these couples provided evidence that infidelity was a highly disruptive midlife event. For some partners effects were unresolved and the relational fallout lingered. Counseling helped, but it could not erase the hurt caused by the transgression. Others, such as Sharonda, found a way to accept what had happened. She and Deon report that their relationship is now stable and relatively happy. Infidelity was not often mentioned. Perhaps it was rare in this sample or it may be that some couples simply accepted outside relationships. Of course, it may also be true that couples were unwilling to discuss such a sensitive topic. However, I do see evidence that some couples *were* willing to broach the topic with their student interviewers, some of whom were daughters and sons. As just one example, consider that in an interview with their daughter, one couple recalled an "almost" affair. As they reminded her, the daughter herself had discovered her father exchanging intimate instant messages with another woman. The affair was apparently aborted and the family seemed determined to talk about the incident openly [#013]. So if affairs are underrepresented in our data, it is also the case that some couples were quite forthcoming.

Grandparent Caregiving: *"I just try to have them know they have a stable place to stay"*

Having cleared decades of active childrearing, some couples accepted responsibility for their grandchildren. But to be included in this category, a couple needed to have major caregiving responsibilities, if not legal custody. In some instances their son or daughter had proven to be an unfit parent. In others, the death of adult offspring or their partners created an acute need that the grandparents felt compelled to fill. Many of our older couples relished the opportunity to play a role in the lives of their grandchildren. Although highly committed, the eight couples included in this category were nevertheless challenged by a wholly unexpected midlife transition.

Nancy and Andy experienced tragedy when their son-in-law was killed in a car accident, leaving their daughter as a single parent of three young children. The kids and their mom soon moved in and Nancy quit her job to help her daughter "get through the difficult time" [#177i]. Nancy describes herself as "physically exhausted." The couple described their life as emotionally stressful and reported that the new lack of privacy greatly curtailed their sexual activity. Having accepted this new reality, the pair were committed to creating for their grandkids, and themselves, a sense of stability. They did so by instituting homework and meal schedules, taking the kids to school every day and meeting them afterwards, and having regular talks around the dinner table.

Lee is a truck driver who is nearing retirement, or "forced retirement" as he puts it, due to his many health problems. During their interview, he seemed vexed and frustrated by his unstable second-oldest daughter, whose children this couple have raised for 11 years. Ann, his stay-at-home spouse, explained that they are committed to raising the grandkids into adulthood if need be. He agreed: "I just try to have them know they have a stable place to stay." But the partners have limited energy and financial resources. The arrangement is taking a toll on the lager family. Dayna, the oldest daughter and interviewer wrote that she was able to "see the pain in both of their eyes." Dayna herself admitted to some ambivalence, noting that the choices her parents have made "displace" her and the other two siblings.

In reviewing the interviews it is impossible to miss the fierce commitment of these caregiver grandparents. Despite the obvious challenges most find the experience to be a source of shared satisfaction and joy. One couple found their plans for midlife had taken an unexpected turn, but they expressed little regret. Having been asked to take custody of their newborn granddaughter two years ago, they "couldn't be happier raising this beautiful little girl."

Intersecting Midlife Challenges

Several of the challenges described by midlife couples overlapped conceptually with the more distinct categories presented in Table 3.1. For example, stories about boomerang kids sometimes included references to "difficulties with adult children," a category described below. "Relational stressors," also described below, co-occurred with any number of the original categories. For example, relational rigidity complicated adjustments to financial hardship, as when an unemployed partner proved unwilling to assume domestic duties. Coders struggled to quantify these more ambiguous sets of midlife changes, but they seemed quite important in the lives (and discourse) of many participants. For that reason they are described in detail in this section.

Difficult Adult Offspring

This midlife change was sometimes easily recognizable in the discourse of our midlife partners. Consider, for example, that several pairs of parents described an adult son or daughter who had repeatedly committed criminal offenses. But other examples overlapped with existing categories of midlife change, as when a child with financial or mental health problems "boomerangs" back to the family home. It was often parental disagreements over how to handle these situations that caused adversity. Raven's family moved from the Navajo reservation to the city. Her mother and stepfather clashed over the future of several of their adult children, including her brother.

> My brother Jarrod is twenty years old and he's a very slow learner. He has been on meds since he was ten years old and when he got to high school, he didn't want to take them anymore. My mom said she is afraid to let him be on his own, which is another reason my parents have arguments. [#013i]

Max and Charlotte reported similar friction when interviewed by Dena, their niece, who observed.

> The second significant stressor in their relationship was their son Max junior. He struggled with learning disabilities and as he grew into his teen years, addiction. My aunt and uncle spent much time trying to negotiate and figure out the best ways to help Max junior move past these issues. [#026i]

Other couples were tested by the health challenges of their adult offspring. Lainey's daughter from an earlier marriage endured 16 surgeries to correct a congenital problem with her hearing. Reginald, her second husband, supported Lainey and his stepdaughter through those difficult years. Later, as the couple entered midlife, their biological daughter developed spinal problems during early adulthood, as well as a near-fatal infection. In middle age they are aware of the accumulated mental health effects of these challenges and the fear of losing one of their kids. But they also argue that these difficulties have made them stronger as a couple [#034i].

Relational Stressors

We defined relational stressors as challenges emanating primarily from the interactions of the partners as opposed to changes connected to their individual qualities (e.g, depressive tendencies) or external forces (e.g., death of a family member). Of course, stress-provoking relational practices often intersected with other midlife challenges. For example, the problems of adult children sometimes triggered interactions that were more conflictual than was typical of the couple. Or the demands of caring for ill parents could reduce the quantity and quality of a couple's communication. However, couples often cited the relationship itself as a prominent source of concern. To the extent possible, I separate out these kinds of adversity in this section.

One subcategory that emerged was *problematic patterns of communication*. As Doug Kelley and I (2009) have written elsewhere, these patterns may have developed over a long period of time, but it is at midlife that they "come to a head." No longer distracted by child rearing and the demanding early stages of careers, couples sometimes confront the reality of dissatisfying communication. Among the dysfunctional forms of communication are poor listening, passive and active verbal aggression, wearing criticism, avoidance of difficult topics, emotional distancing, and mutually-destructive conflict tactics.

Anthony and Lauren have been married for 25 years. In their interview Anthony admitted that he has never responded well to criticism, even the constructive variety. He described himself as a "big baby" and Lauren seems to agree. For her part, Lauren admitted that her approach to criticism could be perceived as cold and unloving. This pattern has been a long-standing source of stress in their relationship, but at midlife they are making adjustments. She is learning to make her point in a more supportive way and he is becoming less reactive [#038i].

Darcy's interview with her parents revealed that "both of my parents need some sort of counseling" to help them make some midlife adjustments.

> My mother explained how my father would take out the stress of his day on her, by becoming short, irritable, and distant. "He would disappear into his office for an entire night … he just wouldn't talk to me and snap at me if he did," she told me. She could always tell that he was acting this way, but he would never acknowledge his behavior. After this interview process I realized that both of my parents need some sort of counseling because there are some big communication problems and the fact that they can't talk to each other without yelling at one other is a problem. [#012]

In more extreme cases, couples described *verbal aggression* and even physical abuse. Carmen had the unique experience of interviewing both her parents *and* her grandparents (abuelito/abuelita) at the same time. The interview revealed that her grandfather had greatly restricted his wife's activities when they were young, largely out of his own insecurity. And to Carmen's surprise, he tearfully admitted physically abusing her several times. Carmen's mother revealed that Carmen's father had *also* been quite controlling at times, using threatening language in response to her plans to return to school and get a job. At midlife, both women stood up to these abusive husbands. They called on members of the extended family for support and followed through with plans to be more independent.

As young men, Carmen's father and her *abuelito* appear to have internalized a virulent and twisted form of *machismo*, one they seem to have renounced in middle and older age. She finds hope in the surprising openness and support of her *familia* and in the tearful words of her repentant abuelito: "If I did not have familia, I would have nothing. Familia is worth more than all the money and diamonds combined. True happiness is found within the heart of each of your family members, especially your wife" [#040].

Relational drift was another source of distress, as couples described "drifting apart," boredom, and waning attraction. Janelle lamented the lack of emotional closeness that had evolved over the years as she immersed herself in motherhood and Brad focused on his career. At midlife, they describe relearning the art of self-disclosure and the challenge of becoming vulnerable again [#130i]. Lauren felt her husband Anthony drifting away from the family as he became overly-invested in work and less engaged in their marriage. He assumed that she would be happy with him continuing to serve as the couple's primary bread winner. But as the kids approached adulthood, she determined to go back to school, seek her own job, and become more independent. These moves shocked Anthony and helped him realize that "if he wanted to keep things together, then he needed to do his part to stay a family" (#038).

Rigidity was the issue for some couples who found in one partner or both an inability to adapt to the changing circumstances of midlife. This was typically described as being "stuck" in old patterns or "locked in" to familiar habits (e.g., watching television every night). A frequent example involved spouses who were unwilling to renegotiate domestic responsibilities when their partners returned to school or accepted more demanding jobs. Other forms of rigidity included unwillingness to accept the limitations of an illness or injury, reluctance to seek change through counseling, and persistence in destructive behaviors such as overwork or excessive purchases.

And finally, *unresolved grievances* were expressed as couples revealed long-held grudges, unaddressed hurt, and resentment. When they were young, Kendra and Sid could afford only one car. After spending a long day at home with their very young daughters, she would drive to the office to pick him up. Absent-minded to a fault, Sid would lose track of time, leaving her waiting in the car for as long as 20–30 minutes. This behavior left Kendra stewing with resentment. Unwilling to accept her own harsh feelings, she left them unexpressed for more than 20 years. Only in her middle age did Kendra realize that she harbored deep resentment about this and other acts of disrespect [personal communication with the author]. The couple confronted the issue. Sid apologized. Together they worked to adopt a more open an respectful approach. Gradually, Kendra has begun to forgive Sid and let go of the old resentments.

Making Sense of Adversity

The challenges described by these midlife couples are many, but they can be condensed along several broad dimensions. The first of these is *severity*. Some of these midlife pairs experienced little, or only mild, adversity in the course of their long relationships. But they were unusual. By my estimate roughly 90% of couples experienced a significant adverse event or serious challenge. That only makes sense. They had lived together for many years and even the most charmed marriage will encounter some very trying times.

For some of these couples, midlife has been characterized by *cascading* challenges. Rufus interviewed Walter and Liz, friends of his family. Here is what he found.

> The last 10 years was very tough for the couple … In this decade, Walter and Liz both lost their jobs and parents and family members. And their family members stole thousands of their money twice. They had to cover the financial losses. Walter's mother was in a nursing home, so they took care of her cats and dogs. Walter got cancer in this decade, which made his back worse. "It has been a very, very, very, very tough 10 years," said Liz. When they were talking about this 10 years, they both spoke in a low, sad voice. And Liz' eyes even turned red. Their expressions are crying-like smiling. It was hard for them to adjust to the challenges.

So, clearly some couples have been more challenged than others. And, as I consider how it is that these couples persisted, I expect that some are worse for the wear, barely coping as the years passed. But creativity is said to be born from adversity, and we will see in later chapters that some relationships are characterized by radical adaptation and even reinvention.

Another way to parse these challenges is by the *social unit* identified as the source of the challenge. Couples reported that some challenges could be attributed to an *individual* member of the couple. Examples include a husband's decision to cheat on his wife or a spouse's decreasing career satisfaction. Sometimes the challenge was attributed to *relational* sources, the joint activities of the partners. Examples include mutually-destructive communication patterns and stale relational routines. The *family*, both nuclear and extended, was sometimes perceived as the source of stress, adversity, or relational disruption, as when an adult child unexpectedly returned home or an ill parent required caretaking. In contrast, many challenges emanated from *societal or cultural* sources. These included stress-provoking changes in the economy (see Chapter 1), an employer's fortunes, or the neighborhood in which the couple lived. Finally, some changes were attributed to *fate*. Couples described being subjected to bad luck, unexplainable circumstances, or changes in "God's plan." Serious illnesses or the death of adult offspring are among the events that were interpreted this way.

Another scheme for classifying these challenges involved time and intensity. *Chronic* challenges were those the couple endured over long periods of time. Examples included certain long-term medical conditions such diabetes or the adult son or daughter who frequently needed financial support. Some couples described long-running relationship patterns, such as disrespectful communication or inattentiveness. *Acute* challenges were short-lived but intense. Examples included unexpected job loss, acts of infidelity, an episode of serious illness, and a difficult relocation. These acute challenges sometimes were the catalyst for long-lasting modifications in relational identity and communication practices, but the event itself was viewed as time-limited. In fact, the term "event" is apt, because some of the challenges were associated with familiar *lifecourse events* such as adult children leaving the home, a stay-at-home spouse returning to the workforce, or the retirement of one or both partners.

Having surveyed the battered landscape of midlife challenges and stressors I now turn to the means by which these couples managed to survive. After all, the remarkable thing about each of these couples is their resilience. Despite the difficulties, they have stayed together—for better and sometimes for worse—for an average of nearly 30 years. They seem to have evidenced an unusual capacity to hang in there over the long run and a strong need to make it to the finish line—together. Ahmed and his wife Malika experienced a long and painful period of geographic separation during their first 25 years of marriage. The time apart made them deeply appreciate their bond. He explained it this way: "The biggest difference is, when we were 25 years old we wanted to love and live with each other, and now that we are 50, we want to die together."

References

Bouchard, G. (2014). How do parents react when their children leave home? An integrative review. *Journal of Adult Development, 21*, 69–79.

Henry, R. G., & Miller, R. B. (2004). Marital problems occurring in midlife: Implications for couples therapists. *The American Journal of Family Therapy, 32*, 405–417. doi:10.1080/01926180490455204

Lodge, A. C., & Umberson, D. (2012). All shook up: Sexuality of mid- to later-life married couples. *Journal of Marriage and Family, 74*, 428–443.

Lucas, K., & Buzzanell, P. M. (2012). Memorable messages of hard times: Constructing short- and long-term resiliences through family communication. *Journal of Family Communication, 12*, 189–208. doi:10. 1080/15267431.2012.687196

Mount, S. D., & Moas, S. (2015). Re-purposing the "empty nest." *Journal of Family Psychology, 26*(3), 247–252.

Waldron, V., & Kelley, D. (2009). *Marriage at midlife: Analytical tools and counseling strategies.* New York, NY: Springer.

Waldron, V. & Kloeber, D. (2009). Relocation at midlife: Marking a new era. In Waldron, V., & Kelley, D. (pp. 179–203). *Marriage at midlife: Analytical tools and counseling strategies.* New York, NY: Springer.

Waldron, V., Vynalek, A., Kloeber, D., Cayentano, C., & Froke, A. (2014, November). *Resilience at midlife: Change, adaptation, and optimization in long marriages.* Chicago, IL: National Communication Association.

· 4 ·

PROTECTING

This chapter identifies practices and relational qualities that, in the view of these couples, make them less vulnerable to the forces that can wreak havoc on a midlife marriage. In the parlance of resilience researchers, these are protective (Kent, Davis, & Reich, 2013) or steeling factors (Rutter, 2007). As we will see in Chapters 5 and 6 respectively, relational resilience can be a process of coping with adversity and it may involve relational transformation and growth. But, here in Chapter 4 I focus on resilience as *resistance* to adversity (see Zautra, 2013). In the experiences of these couples, what are the relational practices that prepared for, "warded off," or even prevented adversity at midlife? As they entered the middle years of the lifespan, what strengths and resources had they cultivated and how did these help them negotiate the challenges and stressors described in Chapter 3? To answer these questions, I worked with my research teams to apply the data analysis methods described in Chapter 8. The result is the set of relational practices presented in Table 4.1 and a succinct set of root metaphors grounded in the phrases reported in Table 4.2.

This search for protective practices could easily become a fool's errand, one that could falter quickly under the weight of an enormous body of research on marital satisfaction and longevity. Indeed for many years researchers have

Table 4.1. Protective practices.

Practice	Description
Enacting resilient identities	Protective relational qualities
Determined	"Stubborn," committed, "sticking with it"
Reliable	Dependable; a "go to" couple; steady
Ready	Prepared, equipped with tools; tested
Loving	Unbreakable emotional bonds; "loves conquers all"
Patient	Willing to wait; unrushed; "taking time"
Truth-telling	Confront reality; discuss uncomfortable topics; clear-eyed
Preserving resources	Judiciousness; "choose your battles"; establish priorities
Broaden the base	Expand social networks; value family and friends
Accept the inevitable	"Go with the flow"; adjust expectations
Check in	The habit of communication; frequent status checks
Regulate emotion	Curb arousal; reinterpret feelings
Practicing faith	Praying together; invoking God's plan; professing faith
Putting in the work	Working hard; "it isn't easy"
Anticipatory collaboration	Planning; working together; voicing concerns

Table 4.2. Protective words and phrases.

Friends	Investing; heavily invested
Soul mates	Sacrifice
Glue; stick together	Prepared; ready,
Stay the course; "hang in there"	Tested;
Thick and thin; better or worse	Real life; not a fairy tale
Peaks and valleys	Grounded
Commitment; agreement	Equality; equal investment
Duty/obligation	God's plan; faith; "let God take control"
Team; teamwork	Solid; united
Work; working together; hard work	Fight; battlers
Flow; "ebb and flow"	"Choose your battles"
Fate; things will work out	Absorb the blow; bounce back
Checking in; touching base	Habits; routines
Curbing; curbing enthusiasm; calming	Justice/respect
Resources; conserve; dig deep down	Fate; things will work out
Preserve, protect; saving	

identified relational and personal qualities, beliefs, emotions, and behaviors that shape the experience of romantic partners. It is certainly not my intent to simply rediscover the bases of relational satisfaction or the dimensions of martial communication. Fortunately, other researchers have updated that literature in recent years (e.g. Kelley, 2012). So I focused the analysis in several ways. First, my chief concern is with identifying protective *relational practices*, rather than the attributes, values or commitments of these couples. So if a couple described, for example, being "committed to the marriage," coders were instructed to set this data aside unless the interview also yielded descriptions of behaviors that enacted commitment, such as renewing wedding vows or pledging to stay together through anticipated hard times. In contrast to Chapters 5 and 6, I exclude non-interactive practices, such as placing money in a savings account, unless the couple explicitly discussed their conversations about this action.

A second focusing criterion was the emphasis on practices that became relevant at *midlife* rather than earlier or later in the course of the relationship. As noted in Chapter 8, the interview protocol incudes questions about midlife and the "last ten years." These sections of the interview were given priority in data analysis. Interviewers also inquired about how the marriage was different "now," compared to earlier times. As interviewers probed the responses they often (certainly not always) surfaced information about the relational assets that helped couples ride out any recent turbulence. As the average participant was in her 50s, "recent" meant middle age.

Third, we were skeptical of answers that appeared to recycle platitudes, such as "you have to be ready to work at marriage" or "communication is everything." These responses seemed to tap "big D" cultural discourses about relational resilience (see Buzzanell, 2010) but my interest is in "little d" discourse, and most centrally with the practices that, in this example, *enact* the work of marriage. Finally, we focused our analysis on the period *prior to* an experience of adversity. In contrast, Chapters 5 and 6 focused on practices that emerged during or after the experience of adversity. Of course, this distinction wasn't always clean. Some practices, such as expressions of solidarity prepared some couples for difficult times while others discovered the practice only after experiencing a threat to their unity.

As we will see, couples described such protective practices as habits of communication, managing conflict, and sharing relational rituals, and (for some) sharing faith. A portion of these are similar to relationship maintenance practices that might be used at any point in the lifecourse (see Canary,

Stafford, & Semic, 2002). But others, such as joining forces with adult off-spring, are possible only later in life. Still others seem uniquely crafted to withstand challenges the couples *expected* to happen at midlife, such as illness or caring for an aging parent. So, with that brief preview let's listen to what these couples had to say.

Protective Practices

Analysis of the interviews and the student reviewer reports yield ten distinct protective practices. The first of these, enacting resilient identities, included many variations, all of which are described below and listed in Table 4.1.

Enacting Resilient Identities

Couples described what might in a different context, be considered traits of personality that fostered resilience, such as determination, grit, and a "can do" approach to life (for a list of resilience-related qualities see Zautra & Hall, 2014). However, to be included in this category, couples had to describe what might be called the personality of their *relationship*—a shared identity that prepared them to face down challenges. So, it wasn't the qualities of a partner that mattered most here, although the characteristics of individuals are certainly important. After a period of depression and couples therapy, Leanne described her husband Jake: "I knew he would stick by me through thick and thin" [#275w]. Later the couple described this sticking together as a practice that they shared, a defining feature of their marriage that had been cultivated and tested through years of sometimes difficult experience.

So we listened for descriptions of qualities the partners purported to share and, for this chapter, those described as protective in some way (although most used different words to describe this aspect of relational resilience).

Determined: *"Determined to stay on our feet"*

Wes and Astrid have been married for 31 years. They talked with their son Clay about their approach to married life. The couple has weathered some serious adversity, including a totally unexpected diagnosis of prostate cancer when Wes was in late 40s. For several years the couple actively battled the illness as Wes received chemotherapy. They recounted that period of life to Clay, suggesting that Astrid "took things in stride and never let it stress her too much." Wes says illness actually strengthened their already tight bonds. How? By midlife they were well-prepared for adversity. They had become "bull-headed and stubborn," refused to give up in the face of challenges, and they actually expected them. "Things will go pear-shaped, things will not always work out," Wes observed. Clay agreed, describing his parents with terms such as "strong" and "ready" [#182i,h].

Astrid and Wes were unusual in their mutual embrace of stubbornness; in most of our interviews that word described a personality flaw of one or both partners. But the word "determined" was used frequently by couples and the students who wrote about them. Twenty five different couples described themselves that way: "Determined to bend but not break." "Determined to keep the marriage going." "Determined to stay on our feet." "Determined to fight through thick and thin." Couples enacted that determination by "sticking by" each other, encouraging, expressing optimism about the future, and declaring their resolve to succeed.

Reliable: *"The couple you go to when you have a problem"*

Reliability was another shared relational quality. Having proven themselves over time, partners came to view themselves as reliable sources of support during times of crisis. They supported *each other* as evidenced in numerous interviews. Having encountered in the past such adversities such as illness or a difficult relocation, partners learned that they could "count on," "rely on" and "trust" their spouses to "be there" for them. Rob said he and his wife Dharma have learned, "to be there for your spouse in hard times just as much you would when times are good" [#181h].

Rex and Alice, married 32 years, were interviewed by their twin daughters Hope and Allie. Their narrative was typical in the sense that the couple's track record of mutual reliance leaves then feeling prepared for whatever life has to offer.

> We discovered not long after moving to Arizona that our oldest daughter had a brain tumor. We had just moved to this new state and we had no real support system … we only had each other to rely on. We were both new to our jobs—and with this unexpected occurrence it placed a lot of stress and strain on our lives and family. [#107h)

But for many couples it was their shared identity as a source of support for their adult offspring, extended family members, or friends that most defined this discourse of reliability. Ricardo interviewed his parents Ella and Martin, the parents of five children—2 biological offspring, 2 from previous marriages, and an adopted boy. Now in their 50s the couple had met such challenges as a move-in in-law, two boomerang kids, a business set back, and Martin's declining health. The solid center of a web of diverse family relationships, the couples say that their peers describe them as "the couple you go-to when there is a problem" [#199].

This idea was expressed in numerous ways as partners described themselves as reliable sources of tangible and emotional support. Bea interviewed her grandparents. Now well into their 80s, Bernie and Ona reflected on their days as middle-aged parents. They expected their adult offspring to earn their way in life, but Bernie and Ona stood ready to help with a *particular* kind of crisis—the breakdown of a car. They always had an extra car ready to lend. We "always had wheels if they needed wheels," Bernie reported as Ona nodded in agreement [#167h].

Ready: *"Prepared for life's peaks and valleys"*

Readiness was another theme as couples described their identities using phrases such as "prepared for life's peaks and valleys," and "prepared now more than ever." But that wasn't always the case. Brianne reported this after interviewing her parents:

> My dad said that he had a particularly hard time dealing with me growing up. He said that it was hard to see his little girl go through life's challenges and that I seemed to grow faster than he was ready for. [#021i]

Couples tended to emphasize that life had made them ready; they were "ready now," and "ready for the future." A substantial minority of these partners reported being "not ready" for the challenges of marriage earlier in the life-course, but they *were* ready at midlife. Thus it seems that experience and maturation were the sources of their preparedness. But some couples described intergenerational transmission, the role of their parents or elders in preparing them for adversity. In her interview, Jeanie recalled that it was her own mother who let her know that marriage would not always be easy. Jeanie was ready for the peaks and valleys of midlife and she prepared her husband to ride them out [#031w].

Loving: *"But, ultimately their love sees them through it"*

Some couples simply cited "loving" as the most important factor in their resilience. Having nurtured their love for many years, couples associated it with strength. Maria has been diagnosed with diabetes, heart disease, and chronic anemia. These chronic conditions seem likely to worsen and she and her partner anticipate new challenges. How will they approach them? Husband Enrique mentions a phrase they use often, the "base of true love." He explained that love is both the foundation and the pillars upon which the future of the couple and their larger family will stand as they help Maria persevere in the face of her health challenges [208h]. Another pair, Del and Ramona were typical of couples who talked about love as the source of strength. To their interviewer (Brit), the couple admitted, "there have been, and always will be bumps in the road, but ultimately their love sees them through it" [#226i]. In each of these cases, it was not simply the *existence* of love that seemed protective. Instead it was the couple's invocation of love that mattered most, as if they cultivated strength by voicing, collectively remembering, and pledging allegiance to the love they shared.

Patient: *"In your patience possess ye your souls"* (Luke 21:19)

Many couples described the key to their longevity as "patience," a term that often brought knowing looks and mirthful chuckles. Consider Lori, a van driver for a school district, and David, who has been a truck driver for over 20 years. The pair recently commemorated their 31st year together. Despite various trials, the longevity of their marriage is considered an achievement, one that Lori attributes to their "patience." Events will test your patience David acknowledged. To make it through you need "love, respect, communication, and lots of patience, and more patience" (The pair exchanged looks and chuckled) [#041w,h].

Jules described the stress he felt as a younger man, supporting a family of four as sole breadwinner. He felt impatience at his slow career progress and considerable self-doubt. A nominal Christian at the time, he came across a bible verse, Luke 21:19 "In your patience possess ye your souls." He and his partner Maggie agreed that this verse has guided them through hard times. They firmly believe that patience will be rewarded, even during the most trying of times. "We knew some things had to change as we were getting older and realizing that we were going to be together for the rest of our lives" [#164]. They are not alone. Drew and Vicky, though unmarried, have been together for 26 years. The African American couple have six adult offspring, three each from previous marriages. "Most of the conflicts we had were due to us having no patience" Drew notes. "Your mom (Vickie) is worse than I am however" he suggested playfully, to his interviewer (Vickie's daughter), "but talking about it made us realize that we needed to work on it together and here we are today," Drew said with a smile on his face. The partners handle adversity more calmly now and they are more patient in finding solutions that work for both of them [#168h].

Truth-telling: *"Find a couple who is older and far advanced ... to tell you the truth"*

Interviews revealed that some couples felt stronger for having confronted truths, sometimes painful ones. Having confronted their shortcomings squarely, they felt emboldened to face whatever realities came there way. "The best advice that I can give from my experience is be honest with your partner. Sometimes it is the hardest thing to do, but it is the glue to a relationship" [#113h]. That was Frank, 63 years old and married for 28 years.

In some cases, this lesson was hard-earned. Couples described the pain they had experienced when discovering that a partner was deceptive about the depth of an addiction, financial mismanagement, or the use of pornography. Bethune and Abe have been married for 25 years, a relationship that has been complicated by the blending of two families, forced career changes, and differences over how to accommodate a boomeranged son. According to Bethune:

> The ability to express how you feel and be open with your thoughts will save a marriage. Even though it might hurt initially, in the long run, your significant other will be grateful you told them the truth. [#098w]

Having avoided direct communication early on, the partners feel better equipped for the challenges they will face in the "long run." Mitch and Judee, a couple in their mid-forties, spent years tiptoeing around tough subjects, using words like "sure" or "whatever you want" to avoid confrontation. "Now," Judee says, "I'll say I don't understand what you're trying to say when you say 'sure'. When we were younger, we wouldn't have done that" [#075w].

Other couples felt stronger because they sought truth from outside sources. In their 26 years of marriage, Martin and Ella have, with the help of others, confronted some uncomfortable truths. Reflecting on this, 55-year-old Martin advised Ricardo, his son and interviewer, to replicate a practice that had helped them endure. "Find a couple who is older and far advanced ... to tell you the truth" [#199h].

Preserving Relational Resources: *"Marriage is a give and give situation"*

Another frequent refrain involved the stewardship of relational resources. Couples suggested that being judicious now would pay-off in the future, when larger challenges might be encountered. In the realm of conflict management, at least ten couples described some version of the phrase "You've got to choose your battles." The underlying rationale seemed to be the preservation of good will and emotional energy. Knowing that arguments could be draining, couples saved their energy for the conflicts that really mattered. In that spirit, Randi's mother said, "little things may bug you but life isn't perfect and there are bigger things to worry about" [098w].

Related ideas involved the investment of resources to build the partner up, make things equal, or stockpile energy for future challenges. "Marriage is a give and give situation," noted Brock who has been married to Kelly for 42 years. As did others, Brock described an ethic of mutual generosity that sustains their marriage over time, a process of "banking" resources for when they are needed. Banking was more than a metaphor for some couples, who regretted squandering funds earlier in their marriage. Charles and Leigh apparently never recovered, much to their regret: "We were never good storers, we give things away, and we're not so good at handling finances. We have wasted too much money in our life time" [#084h]. But for quite a few couples, learning to talk about money was a key to saving it for the future. Gayle and Dray battled over spending habits in the early years of marriage but learned "to communicate with each other when we were spending money, and really making sacrifices, and not spend frivolously" [#114w]. For them, learning to talk about money was a key to saving it for the future, when they would need to cover the costs of health care and unexpected emergencies.

Broadening the Base: *"You need people you can count on in challenging times"*

Couples described brittle support systems that were shored up as they entered midlife, sometimes in response to feelings of loneliness, alienation, or abandonment. The marriage of Beale's parents staggered under the weight of his father's job loss, which lasted more than a year. His parents realized they needed the help of others if they were to survive that kind of experience in the future. "My father strongly believes that being part of a strong support group is also essential, whether it be family, friends or the church. You need to be able to have people you can count on in challenging times" [#160]. Yas and Nascha have reinvigorated their efforts to stay connected to family. Native Americans living off their home reservation, they rediscovered the importance of family ties when Nascha got sick and lost her job. Going forward, they feel bolstered by the support of Nascha's family, and have welcomed their visits [#043].

Accepting the Inevitable: *"The ebb and flow of marriage"*

These midlife couples had ridden out enough ups and downs to be unsurprised by what Astrid described as the "ebb and flow of marriage" [#182w]. They seem determined not to overreact to positive and negative developments, endorsing instead a kind of steadiness. Acceptance was the theme underlying many of these comments. "We feel like we can just be with one another and we don't expect things that will never change," was the comment Thelda offered about her long relationship with Manny. Their interviewer, Gisela, reported that Thelda "no longer expects her husband to change … and she has learned to accept these areas about him. The two also expressed how they are able to talk to each other and there are no hiding meanings or motives, they know they are going to be together and that any issue that arrives is one they will work out together" [#102 i,w,h,]. In a different interview with similar themes, Ona agreed. "We learned the point is to understand, and accept differences. You have to think, is this really so important?" [#167]. Henry and Pia, born in the Phillipines, viewed this tendency through a cultural lens.

> By being mature—by nature, Filipinos are very resilient people. We handle adversities well, because buckling under pressure makes the rest of the family suffer. We have to be strong and go with the flow all the time, and be genuinely happy about it.

In general, couples taking this perspective prided themselves on the ability to "ride out" the occasional wave of gloom, to "work though" the knotty times. As Keith described it:

> … as time goes along, and as you have more history with one another, the peaks and valleys tend not to be as high. So we don't get *as* upset with each other, because we know it is all going to be okay. We are going to work through it and we will figure it out. [#213h]

Checking in: *"for fifteen minutes they speak about … how things have changed around them"*

Many couples pointed to protective effects of their communication practices. Communication was referenced more than 700 times in the interview reports and nearly every one of the 265 couples said something about it. Of course, the student interviewers were enrolled in a communication course at the time of the interview, so they were sensitized to the concept. And frankly, a few interviewees seemed content to share bromides ("Communication is the key") with their student interviewers and leave it at that. Nonetheless, it is clear from these interviews that many couples had learned to communicate differently and better during their middle age. Some of their practices are better described elsewhere in this chapter. See, for example, the sections on truth telling or emotion management. I reserve this section for "habits of communication" (see Waldron & Kelley, 2009), routinized practices that midlife couples believe account for their success during hard times. For further reading on this topic see the literature on the ordinary patterns of communication that serve to maintain relationships (e.g. Canary et al., 2003). Of course, habits of communication are important at *any* point in the lifespan of a relationship. But I focus on those that couples associated with their middle years. These habits were typically formed to replace less successful approaches of the past.

Checking in was such a practices. Couples described having "drifted along" in the past only to be unpleasantly surprised by a "huge misunderstanding," a hidden financial vulnerability, or a major disagreement over adult offspring or caregiving. By touching base regularly, couples stayed abreast of finances and feelings, they "headed off" budding misunderstandings, and they built solidarity (see Chapter 6), so they would be "on the same page" if a crisis emerged. Stephanie and Todd are in their 26th year of marriage, the second time for each of them. Stephanie confided to her interviewer, Sadie. Having been married previously and unsuccessfully, she explained, the partners have learned from their past. They know that differences of opinion can develop, and what was true last week may not apply today. "So they both sit down in the morning and for fifteen minutes they speak about their politics and how things have changed around them" [#217i].

During their early years together, the marriage of Lei and Fei was threatened by his infidelity. The relationship barely survived and eventually the couple sought counseling. Among the improvements was a new habit of touching base regularly. To exemplify this, the pair noted that an adult son was now living at home. The couple discusses his status frequently, sharing views on his progress toward independence and monitoring their own mixed feelings about his presence. In this and other areas of their marriage, frequently touching base helps avoid unpleasant surprises and emotional blow-ups [#036i]. Manuela suffered from depression early in her married years and at midlife she remains scarred by a childhood of abuse. Manuela has refused to seek counseling or even speak directly about the abuse. Her marriage to Miguel has suffered at times, but she does find strength and certainty in the routines of daily conversation. In recent years, her daughter reports that her parents have committed to chat every day, "with just them alone, to talk about their daily routines and what is on each other's mind. They started doing this not too long ago and up till now it seems to be working."

Regulating Emotion: *"You can't just blow your top off, walk out the door"*

Regulating emotion is a practice that appears to improve in middle and later life (Greve & Staudinger, 2006) and it is likely to have protective effects. One dimension of this practice is curbing arousal (see also Waldron & Kelley, 2009, p. 46). Some of our couples recognized a tendency to overreact during times of crisis, so they prepared themselves by keeping stress at manageable levels, and by identifying, voicing, venting, or rechanneling emotions. Knowing that upcoming events might trigger emotional reactions, partners rehearsed their responses and crafted communication rules to keep emotions in check. "You can't just blow your top off, walk out the door," Barb acknowledged. As did several other couples, she and Brock have learned to anticipate and process their emotions in advance of challenging conversations. In their case, that conversation is likely to center on Brock's desire to return to work after retiring at Barb's request [#058].

Managing stress was often the focus of these arousal management conversations. A familiar discussion topic was the effects of overwork and career-related stress. For example, Lee and Ann know that the stress of his job makes him more volatile which in turn hampers their conversations with an adult daughter for whom they provide extensive childcare. The couple is discussing ways to lower their expenses, so Lee can retire soon [#024]. The money they spend on childcare is for them a "hot topic." But not all arousal management efforts are focused on controlling negative emotions. Mandy reported that her parents were very excited about playing the role of grandparents, even if that opportunity appeared to be a distant glimmer. During the interview her father gushed, "I absolutely love the idea of grandchildren! I love kids when they are little and I love kids when they aren't as little." As was apparently typical, at this point his spouse (Vanessa) interjected to curb his enthusiasm. She worried about interfering in the lives of their adult children and cautioned Graham that his excessive excitement could be interpreted as pressure to have children.

Another emotion management practice was reframing. Anticipating difficult times ahead, partners collaborated to reinterpret emotions in a manner that facilitated rather than inhibited an adaptive response. Joaquin was unpleasantly surprised to learn that his unmarried oldest daughter was pregnant and he dreaded the conversation he would have with her. "I was very sad at first," he confessed. But he and Sofia discussed his feelings and Joaquin was reminded that, "my parents always told me to always look in the light of the situation; my wife and I were going to be grandparents." He ended up feeling joyful in his new role as grandfather.

Practicing Faith: "You pray more, you lean on God more"

Many of the 265 couples in this sample credited their religious faith for protecting them from adversity. In some cases, individual partners saw themselves as stronger, braver, taller, when feeling connected to God. Seth's father, a devout Mormon, advised him: "Stay close to the Lord. A man is never taller than when he is on his knees" [154h]. He was not alone in this sentiment. "I wasted about 20 years in my life without knowing Christ," said Charles. His faith makes him better prepared for challenges that knocked him off course when he was younger. More pertinent to our topic, the practice of faith was often collective, enacted through shared study or prayer. Seth's parents "pray together every night and read the Book of Mormon together." He observed, "I realize this is all very religious but in my parents eyes religion is the reason they've been able to stay together for as long as they have" [#154h,i]. The resilience-enhancing benefits of shared faith was a prominent theme. Ronald and his spouse Nancy "keep God in the center of our marriage." Ronald went on to say, "Marriage is very difficult and staying married is not easy. Bad things happen. Kids born with birth defects, job losses, health scares, the very most important thing is to have a common value system with your partner" [160h]. Dharma offered similar testimony about the role of shared faith in alleviating struggle at midlife:

> Through all trial and tribulations, you get to know one another better. We work through things easier now in which we struggled with before. You pray more, you lean on God more, especially when you know he's the one that brought you and your loved one together. [#181w]

Relabeling Marriage: *"She is my sweetie, best friend, and soul mate"*

For a segment of our sample, "marriage" was an insufficient label, one that failed to fully capture the strengths they brought to their midlife relationship.

The most common alternative was "best friends," although some partners called themselves "soul mates." Ron used both terms to describe his relationship with Nan. "She is my sweetie, best friend, and soul mate. We have gone through so many up's and down's but we always turn to each other and keep God in the center of our marriage" [#160h]. These labels connoted permanence, an unbreakable connection, and resilience in the face of adversity. Gene and Teresa were both married previously and divorced, but their 22nd anniversary was approaching at the time of the interview. In their early 60s now, the partners view their marriage as a deep friendship. Teresa mused: "as we grow older, a lot of it is just enjoying each other and being comfortable together. We really are best friends and we remain best friends as the years go on, and that's what is important. Every morning we enjoy a cup of coffee, read our books and the bible together and at night we enjoy a nice cocktail and play card games together" [183w].

Landon and Marla have been together since the age of 15. At 19 he quit a rock band to join Marla as she took a job in far-away city. They were interviewed by their daughter (Marissa) who describes them as "best friends." The people in their social group also view them as best friends. And it almost goes without saying that John and Marla say they are "inseparable" and yes, "still best friends" after 27 years of marriage. Marissa observes the couple's day-to-day behavior:

> If they can't be together they talk and text all day long and keep in touch with what each other is doing. Any sort of distance between them actually makes them strong because they miss each other even after a day because they are so used to spending every minute together.

But even this companionate couple has faltered, admitting a "close call with divorce" of which Marissa was unaware. Looking ahead, the couple assured Marissa they will get through the worst of times because they belong together. As Marla explained, "We don't know who we are without each other, or what to do if we're not together" [141i,w].

Noel and Pam "met through friends when they were attending a wedding together, then things seemed to get out of control, at least for Joel, [who ended up] drinking sake from a shoe by the end of the night. Pam was then forced to take care of him the rest of the night, stating that she thought to herself 'who is this crazy man?'" [#147i]. These words are from Carmen, drawing from an interview with her parents, a couple whose middle years have been crazy too, but for darker reasons. Pam has endured a series of serious health conditions, including cancer. And Joel's business has ridden a dizzying series of ups and downs. Time and again Pam has needed full-time caregiving and Joel has taken up to a month from his work so he could be at her side. The couple knows the future will also be rocky. As the interview drew to a close, Carmen notes:

> The only thing they had left to say was that they believed they were truly with their soul mates. And if all that has happened had happened with someone else, the relationship wouldn't have lasted. They are both extremely strong and could handle everything in a way that showed support and that they wouldn't give up. The last statement Joel said was, "I'm just glad we met each other and are still able to love each other."

Putting in the Work: "Marriage is not easy. It takes work!"

Couples often cited the familiar refrain, "Marriage is work," emphasizing that it takes considerable effort to stay together over the long term. But underlying this trope was an understanding of work as a protective practice. Indeed, some interviewees saw relational work as long distance runners or swimmers think of practice. For them, intensive practice, "putting in the work," builds the muscle and endurance that comes in handy at "crunch time." "Work hard!" urged Bernie [#167h]. "Do not give up!" Micki exclaimed, sharing the mantra that guided her though the trying periods of a 31-year marriage to Bill [#192i]. After interviewing his parents, whose marriage had been battered at midlife by a storm of challenges, including his father's alcoholism, Pedro concluded that they are now "invincible." His father explained that "life is not always easy," but "you will get through the bad times" if you work to make them easier, as had he and Alma.

Building on this theme of hard work, interviewees frequently claimed that marriage is not easy. Indeed, the phrase "not easy" appeared in dozens of interviews. "Marriage is not easy. It takes work," agreed Larry and Sally, married 38 years. Silas brought his aging parents from Nigeria to live in the home he shared with Akira. "This was not easy … You have to find a way to work this out with your spouse and your children." The upshot for many partners was the understanding that by working hard at marriage, they became stronger, better able to go the distance. Faith and Steve were asked to describe how their marriage is different now, at midlife. Their daughter Stephanie summarized the response.

> Their marriage is still the same but also different. It's the same because they rely on each other for various different reasons and they both work hard to provide a life for

each other in the good and bad times. It's also different because of the history they share together … they are now stronger as a couple. [204i]

Anticipatory Collaboration: *"We talk about everything as a family"*

Collaboration and cooperation are presumably the touchstones of any long relationship. Most of these midlife couples described efforts, sometimes heroic ones, to synchronize their goals, schedules, and activities. But some collaborative efforts stood out because the partners undertook them to ward off anticipated threats to the marriage or the larger family unit to which they belonged. Over and above its role as the basic mechanism by which inter-dependence is expressed, this brand of purposeful collaboration appeared to have protective effects.

Silas and Akira, the couple who brought his Nigerian mother into their home, are a case in point. With two kids still at home they recently welcomed back their oldest son who has had trouble finding a job. The house is now quite crowded and the couple anticipated that current tensions might lead to future hostilities. In their interview with Moji, the couple described pur-poseful collaboration. First, having anticipated their son's return, the couple were able to "game plan" (Moji's term) the situation so they would not be overwhelmed by it. Second, they instituted the practice of family meetings, when any member of the family is encouraged to voice concerns. Third, Silas reported:

> We talk about everything as a family and come up with resolutions to resolve issues. We attend community events together as well as going on family vacations. All these things helped us to adjust and remain unified as things continuously changed around us. [#015h]

A second theme emerging here is another variation on "working." Unlike its usage above, working in this context means collaborating to improve the system so it is "working smoothly," or "running on all cylinders." By work-ing things out, partners made their marriage ready for the future and avoided breakdowns at critical junctures. The last ten years of marriage have been rough on Blaine and Tonie. They "could have walked away and quit," she observed, but now "we have all the little kinks worked out" [159w]. As did so many other couples, Kent and Eileen felt better prepared for the future because they had learned to collaborate in the past. As Kent nodded, Eileen explained that the marriage was "stronger because we had to work together to pull through" [#033w].

Root Metaphor Analysis

The taxonomy of protective practices proved to be quite extensive. In the interests of parsimony, I used root metaphor analysis (see Chapter 9) to iden- tify several primary sense-making schemes used by couples as they reflected on their capacity to weather the challenges of midlife. Table 6.2 lists many of the phrases and figurative forms of speech that we identified while analyz- ing the interviews for protective practices. Of course, in framing this chapter around "protective" factors, I have invoked a metaphor favored by resilience researchers (for a critical analysis of resilience metaphors, see Pizzo, 2015). This particular metaphor implies that certain qualities are inherent to, or can be acquired by, partners who will be shielded from harm. The metaphor can be faulted for overestimating the extent to which the effects of certain kinds of adversity (e.g., cancer) can be avoided and underestimating the costs of protective efforts, such as expensive preventive care. Interestingly, protection was not an *explicit* theme in the discourse used by the couples we interviewed. Instead, several other root metaphors were expressed.

The first of these was "grounded." This metaphor was sometimes used explicitly ("Grounded in our years together") but more commonly its mean- ing was expressed through a cluster of related terms, such as "solid," "reliable," "steady," "strong' "tested" and "prepared" and "mature." All of these descrip- tors suggest that the relationship has accumulated strength, become durable, grown deep roots. Having survived the passing of many years, having healed the inevitable scars, these couples see themselves as ready for anything that comes their way. The image of a mature, weather-scarred oak comes to mind. These couples seem firmly rooted but they also approach challenges with a certain sense of dignity and equanimity. The protective practices that seem associated with this metaphor include a number of the relational identities enacted in the discourse of these couples: determined, reliable, and ready. The practice of managing emotion, particularly the curbing of arousal can be fit here, as volatility is in opposition to groundedness. Looking further, for at least some couples, this grounding is in the firmament of shared faith and for many others rooted in a broadened base of social support.

Another prominent metaphor equates the relationship to an *unbreak- able bond*. These couples attribute their strength in the face of adversity to a deep sense of connection. These partners relabel their relationship, equat- ing it to an enduring friendship or the spiritual connection shared by soul mates. They talk about the "glue" that binds them, finding it in the form of deep love, truth-telling, lasting commitment, and a patience born of genuine understanding. The practice of checking in applies here, because frequent communication is interpreted as evidence that the partners are indeed inseparable. This root metaphor extends to the idea of the couple as a "team," committed to working together, to working things out. The practice of anticipatory collaboration flows from this understanding. Having collaborated closely for years, these couples stay connected during periods of adversity that would fray the bonds of more ordinary relationships.

The root metaphor of *flow* was a less dominant but still notable presence in this body of relational discourse. Couples had learned to "ride out" life's ups and downs, to accept reality, to be comfortable with the truth. This perspective informed efforts to be judicious with resources, to avoid wasting emotional energy and good will, to "pick your battles," to recognize that things "would work out," to let things "balance out." By being good stewards of relational resources these couples seemed to be saying, they would be calmer, more focused, and better supplied for those moments when they needed to actively resist forces that genuinely threatened them. I note as well that for religious couples a sense of peace and confidence came from accepting what they viewed as "God's plan."

In contrast, consider a fourth root metaphor, which was perhaps narrower in its meaning but frequently invoked, *marriage as work*. From this understanding, partners would overcome adversity because they had prepared for it. Relationships were "not easy," but hard work built on a foundation of understanding and compromise that left partners in a strong position at midlife, more likely to prevail than in the effortless, carefree days of their youth. The work metaphor suggests that relational muscles can be built from the ingredients of practice and focused effort. It emphasizes the agency of relational actors, the tractability of most relational challenges, and an optimistic belief that every couple can prevail, if they just choose not to give up. In these assumptions, the marriage as work metaphor may be most closely tied to the idea that defined this chapter, that certain practices offer protection from relational adversity.

Analysis and Conclusions

In this chapter, as I will in Chapters 5 and 6, I let the couples speak with minimal assistance from the literature. The idea was to privilege the voices of those who have lived into midlife and managed to stay together, sometimes against considerable odds. Their long experience has earned them a certain credibility. Of course, much of their experience (certainly not all) can be described more succinctly in the language of established theory and I want to explore some of those theoretical connections as I close this chapter. First, we see in this data evidence of the ways in which couples talk normalcy into being (Buzzanell, 2010). That is, by the way they recount their histories, their mastery over troubles of the past, these couples define the strengths they bring to the present moment. In this chapter we saw couples who defined themselves as determined, reliable and prepared. This a discourse of readiness. By sharing it with these young interviewers partners affirmed (to themselves) their relational preparedness and invited an intergenerational discourse that may be renewed in the relationships of my students.

Expressing determination is no guarantee that one will act in a determined manner. But, these couples provided ample evidence that the discourse of readiness has translated into action. And many described practices that appeared consistent with this way of speaking. For example, one couple was planning for the day when her advancing illness would mean he would leave his work to be there every day as her caretaker. Other couples were hatching plans to help their struggling adult offspring while still preserving their own financial and emotional resources. The couple who was, even now, seeking counseling in anticipation of the friction that would accompany their retirement—they too are examples of readiness translated to action.

Concrete action must be taken to prepare for the unexpected set back or unanticipated hardship. But some evidence indicates that identity may drive that action. In a study of survivors of brain injury, those who adopted the identity of a survivor appeared to be more active in promoting their own well-being, more satisfied with life (Jones et al., 2011). In the current study, many couples described resilient identities informed by metaphors of groundedness and strong bonds. We don't know if these self-conceptions explain why couples persisted into midlife and I didn't measure their sense of well-being. But, having reviewed hundreds of these interviews, I can report that the couples themselves see those connections. And many described concrete behaviors that enacted this view of themselves. One advantage of a long track record is that the partners "know the score" and they are inclined to "tell it like it is." So, among the key findings of this chapter is that the discourse of relational identity may in itself have protective effects, perhaps by motivating couples to engage in behaviors that make them more resistant to adversity.

The relationship maintenance literature emphasizes ordinary communication practices that keep relationships stable and viable (Canary et al.,

2002). Certainly, we see evidence of those behaviors in such practices as "checking in." In previous observations of midlife couples, Douglas Kelley and I (2009) argued that those who had failed to establish patterns of voluntary and routine communication were disadvantaged when they were *required* to communicate to address a conflict, clear up a misunderstanding, or negotiate new relational norms. One explanation might be a practice effect due to years of regular dialogue. At midlife, couples may be harvesting the fruits of their communicative labors or, alternatively, suffering the consequences of a long history of neglect. Certainly, the couples who developed apparently healthy habits of communication seemed confident that they would prevail in the face of midlife challenges.

The routinization of certain kinds of communication may free resources that can be used for more creative problem solving. This may also be true of emotion management. We saw evidence of couples working together to curb negative emotions and replace them with more positive ones. Recall the father who, in anticipation of a difficult conversation with his daughter about her out-of-wedlock pregnancy, was convinced to replace feelings of sadness with joy. It was his wife and family members who prompted this transformation, evidence that emotion is often produced by collective action. Frederickson's (2001, 2013) broaden-and-build theory posits that negative emotions activate regions of the brain associated with highly-focused, short term, and routinized responses. These are useful when facing a clear and immediate threat, but less helpful when the threat is diffuse and more creative responses are required. In contrast, positive emotions activate regions of the brain associated with more creative and adaptive responses. The actions taken by some of our couples may indicate a certain broaden-and-build tendency at the relational level—a proposition worth exploring with additional research.

The practices we observed in these long term couples seem to involve judicious allocation of relational resources. This ethic of stewardship is consistent with models of resilience at the community level (Desouza & Flanery, 2013; Pizzo, 2015). In theory, communities that conserve such assets as talent, financial resources, and even goodwill are more prepared for a crisis. However the capacity to collaborate, to make decisions that are responsive to a broad range of interests is also important. Collaboration is a means by which resources are allocated, or during a period of adversity, reallocated. In our data, we see evidence that these couples collaborated before problems arose, presumably creating the capacity to solve problems when they arose. The creation of collaborative problem-solving processes has emerged as a key to resilience in other contexts, including families and stepfamilies (Golish, 2003; Langford, 2015).

Building on this idea, it appeared that some couples drew protection from their capacity to anticipate problems, often based on past experience. They "worked hard" to create the compromises that made them resistant to potentially damaging conflicts and they treated unhealthy illusions with doses of truth-telling. In the parlance of safety engineers, they created a fail-safe system. Of course, to meet the fail-safe standard, designers need to anticipate every imaginable threat, a practical impossibility in most cases. An alternative to this approach has been emerging in recent discussions of emergency preparedness and community design. What if instead of fail-safe, structures and communities were designed to be "safe-to-fail" (see Wharton, 2015 for a synopsis of one recent project). What if instead of building the tallest and thickest dam to stop a 1000 year flood, residents simply built their houses on stilts and community parks were positioned in flood zones, so water could sweep through with little impact?

I would argue that in outlook and action, some of our couples have designed safe-to-fail relationships. They can't possibly anticipate all the challenges that could come their way, but they know that challenges are likely (see Connolly, 2015 for similar ideas grounded in study of resilience within lesbian couples). Rather than embrace what they have come to see as unrealistic expectations, they have adopted more accurate ones. They conserve their emotional resources and "go with the flow." Rather than interpret each crack in the relationship as a design flaw, they rethink the design, choosing an approach that better matches the changing landscape of midlife. They rely on the support of others. They wait to see how things will work out, even as they touch base frequently and practice the kinds of collaborative problem-solving that is truly valuable in a crisis. In the end, the term "protective factors" fails to fully capture the diverse array of practices that allows these couples to manage adversity. They do not so much shield themselves from the occasional wave of distress that sweeps through nearly every midlife marriage; instead they have perfected the art of stepping aside as it rushes on by.

References

Buzzanell, P. M. (2010). Resilience: Talking, resisting, and imagining new normalcies into being. *Journal of Communication*, 60(1), 1–14.

Canary, D. J., Stafford, L., & Semic, B. A. (2002). A panel study of the association between main-tenance strategies and relational characteristics. *Journal of Marriage and Family, 64*, 395–406.

Connolly, C. M. (2005). A qualitative exploration of resilience in long-term lesbian couples. *The Family Journal, 13*(3), 266–280.

Desouza, C., & Flanery, T. H. (2013). Designing, planning, and managing resilient cities: A conceptual framework. *Cities, 35*, 89–99.

Fredrickson, B. (2013). Positive emotions broaden and build. *Advances in Experimental Social Psychology, 47*, 1–53.

Fredrickson, B. L. (2001). The role of positive emotions in positive psychology: The broaden-and-build theory of positive emotions. *American Psychologist, 56*(3), 218–226.

Golish, T. (2003) Stepfamily communication strengths: Understanding the ties that bind. *Human Communication Research, 29*, 41–80.

Greve, W., & Staudinger, U. M. (2006). Resilience in later adulthood and old age: Resources and potentials for successful aging. In D. Cicchetti & A. Cohen (Eds.), *Developmental psychopathology, Vol. 3: Risk disorder, and adaptation.* (2nd ed., pp. 796–840). Hoboken, NJ: Wiley.

Jones, J. M., Haslam, S. A., Jetten, J., Williams, W. H., Morris, R., & Saroyan, S. (2011). That which doesn't kill us can make us stronger (and more satisfied with life): The contribu-tion of personal and social changes to well-being after acquired brain injury. *Psychology & Health, 26*(3), 353–369.

Kelley, D. K. (2012). *Martial communication.* Cambridge, UK: Polity Press.

Kent, M., Davis, M. C., & Reich, J. W. (Eds.). (2013). *Handbook of resilience approaches to stress and trauma.* New York, NY: Routledge.

Langford, J. (2015, August 14). Family resilience. *Presentation to the City Club of Cleveland.* Retrieved from https://www.youtube.com/watch?v=A0TPxnkJYe0

Pizzo, B. (2015). Problematizing resilience: Implications for planning theory and practice. *Cit-ies, 43*, 133–140.

Rutter, M. (2007). Resilience, competence, and coping. *Child Abuse, & Neglect, 31*, 205–209.

Waldron, V. R., & Kelley, D. (2009). *Marriage at midlife: Counseling strategies and analytical tools.* New York, NY: Springer.

Wharton, K. (2015, July 21). *Resilient cities: Changing the way we think about urban infra-structure* [Press release]. *ASU News.* Retrieved from https://asun̲ow.asu.edu/content/resilient-cities-changing-way-we-think-about-urban-infrastructure

Zautra, A., & Hall, S. (2014). *Resilience solutions group.* Retrieved from http://www.asu.edu/xed/resilience/learnabout.html

Zautra, A. J. (2013). Resilience is social, after all. In Kent, M, Davis, M. C., & Reich, J. W. (Eds.). *Handbook of resilience approaches to stress and trauma* (pp. 185–196). New York: Routledge.

· 5 ·

COPING

Some of our midlife couples describe periods, sometimes *long* periods, when the relationship was sputtering along, held together by a thread (or simply a marriage contract). During these periods they tried to rebuild trust, practiced new communication behaviors, renegotiated rules of engagement, or simply allowed time to heal emotional wounds. In interviews, our participants had much to say about how they coped with such crises as sexual infidelity or serious health problems. They described efforts to normalize at least some aspects of their relationship, even in the midst of disruption, stress, and adversity. Chapter 5 focuses on practices they associated with coping and recovery.

Table 5.1 summarizes these coping practices. As will be the case in Chapter 6, I distinguish emergent practices (those constructed to cope with current difficult circumstances) from protective practices, discussed in Chapter 4. The latter tended to be preventative and anticipatory—the habits and practices that help couples resist stress and adversity. The former were more likely to be reactive, crafted in response to the challenges of the current moment. I further distinguish *communication-intensive adjustments* (e.g. improved listening) from *direct actions* (e.g., seeking a marriage counselor). Drawing on the methodology described in Chapter 8, I also analyze the metaphors used by couples as they talk about their efforts to cope with challenges. Indeed, the

Table 5.1. Coping practices.

Practice	Description
Communication-Intensive Adjustments	
Reestablishing solidarity	"Getting back on the same" page; creating a unified response
Expressing assurance	Reassuring partner of commitment; express support
Honing communication	Improved listening, changed tone of voice; share emotions; talk
Sharing Stories	War stories; funny stories; gaining strength from past triumphs
Recalibrating expectations	Curbing unrealistic expectations; clarifying values and roles
Accepting difference	Making peace with differences; accepting reality
Re/discovering assets	Drawing on personal and relational qualities; calling in favors
Forgiving and reconciling	Addressing hurt; setting conditions; redemption, restoring trust
Escaping	Leaving; seeking respite; taking a break
Managing boundaries	"Walling off" stressors; imposing limits in family relationships
Taking time	Offering to let time pass; seeking perspective; "one day at a time"
Direct Action	
Reallocating work	Work more or differently to relieve stress or dissatisfaction
Seeking help/support	Using public or church-provided services; self-help groups
Re/establishing routines	Resuming or starting rituals; imposing order; normalizing

discourse of coping is rich in symbolic resources as evident in couples' use of such colorful phrases as "getting on the same page," "righting the ship," "keeping the wolves at bay," "getting back on track." Late in this chapter I share a list of these expressions and propose a parsimonious set of root metaphors that informs the language of coping.

Coping refers to the cognitive, emotional, and behavioral efforts people expend to manage or ameliorate stress. In exploring coping in these midlife couples, I am guided by a large body of existing work. This includes models of coping generally (Lazarus & Folkman, 1984), and analyses of coping and aging (Ouwehand, de Ridder, & Bensing, 2007). I also rely on research on the sense-making role that relational narratives play at midlife (Lilgendahl & McAdams, 2011; 2014; McAdams, Reynolds, Lewis, Patten, & Bowman, 2001), analyses of the relational discourse that families use to facilitate coping and resilience during times of adversity (Lucas & Buzzanell, 2012), and recent theorizing on coping as one element of resilient responses to stress and trauma (for a review see Kent et al., 2013). Zautra's (2009, 2013) work on the social dimensions of resilience has also been helpful in this regard.

Much existing work examines coping at the individual level of analysis. In contrast, I want to understand coping as a *relational* process. Similarly, resilience can be conceptualized at the level of the individual, but from the work of Zautra (2013) and others we learn that over and above its genetic, biological, and psychological elements, resilience is a social process—one that succeeds or fails due to the nature of our relationships with others. So, while coping and resilience are certainly shaped by the qualities and choices of individuals, we know that partners travel together through large parts of the lifecourse and their happiness is highly interrelated (Hoppmann, Gerstorf, Willis, & Schaie, 2011). So the focus here is on coping practices that couples enact together and the relational metaphors that they share.

I suggest relational coping is an activity that attempts to stabilize a relationship after disruption, adversity, stress, or trauma. Coping practices deal with adversity in a way that allows people to "muddle through," "keep it together," "hang in there"—to keep the relationship going even if it is temporarily diminished. Coping manages and sometimes ameliorates stress, or at least keeps it at bay, until circumstances improve. Surviving rather than crumbling under the weight of adversity—that is another way to describe coping. In contrast to the thriving/optimizing practices described in Chapter 6, coping typically involves adjustments and relational recalibrations, but perhaps not a relationship transformation. It certainly can involve relational growth, but most often it is growth of the incremental kind. Coping may also be equated with *sustaining* a relationship through a difficult period, the conservation and stewardship of relational resources that may be at risk of depletion. Coping may be an interim step in the larger process of relational resilience, one that sets in motion processes of growth, and even thriving.

The question guiding this chapter is *How?* How do midlife couples cope with adversity? To be included in this part of the analysis, couples must have experienced adversity, disruption, or challenge at midlife. They must have *talked about* how they dealt with it.

Communication-Intensive Practices

Communication practices were often referenced when couples described midlife adjustments. In some cases it was their communication that *required* adjustment. Poor communication skills became evident during a period of adversity and change was required if the couple was to manage. In other cases, couples used communication practices to enact coping responses, such as establishing solidarity or offering assurance. In this way, communication was a tool, or perhaps a symbolic resource, used by couples to deal with adversity.

Reestablishing Solidarity: *"Together is no longer a word, but a way of life"*

Faced with a potentially divisive crisis, such as the unexpected return of adult offspring, partners coped by discovering (or more typically, *rediscovering*) a common voice. Threats to solidarity took a variety of forms. For example, one couple described being "out of synch" when faced with requests for money from adult children or relatives. In the case of boomerang children, parents would sometimes communicate conflicting messages about how long their offspring could stay, how much the son or daughter should contribute for rent, and what household rules might apply. These differing viewpoints exacerbated what was already a stressful situation. To cope, couples hashed out common positions in conversations that were sometimes "difficult" or "very honest." Going forward they would be committed to a unified position until the home was once again their own. Sometimes the situation remained less than ideal, but a united front made it more tolerable by reducing conflict and what Enrique's parents labeled a "competition" for their offspring's affection [#208h].

Jeanie and Paul have been married for 25 years. In the last ten years they have been challenged by serious disagreements on such matters as disciplining their kids. They have learned the hard way that "if you don't stay on the same page it can cause friction" in the family. For them, "together is no longer a word, but a way of life" [#31w]. Doug and Debbie reported that in recent years they coped better with challenging situations because they were mindful about finding a consensus. Doug reported: "We don't make any decisions without praying about it first. If either of us does not get a confirming feeling we do not go through with it" [189h].

Expressing Assurances: *"The relationship was a priority, no matter what obstacles they faced"*

Several of the coping practices resembled relationship maintenance behaviors commonly used by couple at all stages of the lifecourse (Canary, Stafford, & Semic, 2002). Among these is communicating assurances. Assurance may be particularly important at midlife because, for many people, there first encounters with serious illness occur then. A diagnosis of cancer can upend a couple's plans and create uncertainty about the future. A year ago a doctor found an abnormality in Aisha's breast and recommended surgery. "It was the first real health scare we had in our immediate family," she explained. She told us that husband Jamar had trouble coping: "When one of his 'team members' is down Jamar doesn't know how to manage." Jamar's anxiety made the situation more difficult for his wife. Fortunately, Aisha is a nurse and she was able to calm Jamar by explaining the surgery and emphasizing the likelihood of a full recovery [#141w].

Other events, such as job loss, unnerved some midlife couples. Having made a decades-long investment in their work skills, some partners experienced lengthy periods of unemployment and questioned their future in a changing workplace. Ana lost her long-time job in her late forties. Her three children had left home by this time and she wanted to relocate to a more favorable market. But her husband Luis had worked for the same company for 25 years and he was reluctant. The couple argued ferociously over what to do and Ana feared for both the marriage and her career. But ultimately the couple decided that "the relationship was a priority … no matter what obstacles they faced." Luis assured his wife that he would call in favors to help his wife find employment and they worked together to cut back on expenses. Ana felt reassured that the couple would prevail. They did [#178w].

Honing Communication Skills: *"You catch more flies with honey"*

In attempting to ride out a period of relational turbulence, some couples coped by honing their communication skills. Perhaps the most common adjustment involved improvements in listening, but learning to curb criticism was another frequently mentioned practice. Having weathered a period of marital distress, one participant realized that pointed criticism of her husband only made things worse. She started consciously offering him more compliments, a strategy which reduced his tendency to withdraw during this stressful period. "You can catch more flies with honey," she offered [#31w]. Ann has learned that delivering bad news gently helps her husband cope with it. She has "dropping the bomb" down to a science and that keeps Ken's blood pressure in check.

Saundra's mother communicated through "hints," she told her interviewer, Brittany. "She could say, 'Wow, the grass is sure getting long. And Dad could interpret that as 'I need to get out and mow the grass'." At midlife, Saundra came to realize that her husband Kevin needed more direct communication. Kevin's work schedule had become less predictable with a new promotion, but the change was wreaking havoc on the couple's personal life, resulting in cancelled family visits and work calls that disrupted weekends. Saundra grew irritable and the couple quarreled. Finally, she asked Kevin to return to his more predictable work role, even if it meant a reduction in income. He agreed. According to Saundra, her being more assertive saved the relationship considerable stress.

Reginald and Lainey were distressed when, due to an illness, his mother moved into their home for several months. Caregiving drained them both and quiet resentments began to build. As the days wore on tempers flared. The couple realized that unspoken expectations and unexpressed hard feelings were causing a stressful situation to become worse. Perhaps for the first time, the veteran partners agreed to speak more openly about topics that were previously taboo, such as Lainey's conflict with her mother-in-law. This "new openness" helped them understand how caregiving stresses were taking a toll and that resulted in more task sharing and a "stronger bond between them." The mother-in-law is long gone, but the improved communication is an integral part of their relational narrative [#34].

Sharing Stories, Dark and Light: *"Find happiness in this crazy world"*

War stories, whether in the literal or figurative sense, can promote resilience (Socha & Torres, 2015). Stories are vehicles for sharing lessons learned and they can position the tellers as sages, survivors, or heroes. Stories of triumph over adversity are evidence that a person or a couple, had the "right stuff" back then, and perhaps they have it now. Stories of hard times are a kind of discourse that talks normality "into being" (Lucas & Buzzanell, 2012). Our interviews practically invited couples to tell relational war stories and they often accepted the invitation. In fact many used the language of war to describe the hard times they endured together. The husband who battled drug and alcohol addiction. A wife who battled cancer. The couple who fought through the loneliness of an unwanted relocation. The pair that described surviving epic fights that could have derailed the marriage.

We found evidence that couples deploy these stories in times of stress. For example, Eric and Melissa, a couple in their mid-fifties, recently relocated from their beloved home in the Midwest to a remote small town in the desert. This move has been challenging but during the interview they reminisced about an earlier relocation. That one was very stressful too. Their adopted children were quite young and the couple had no friends in the new community. Although they struggled at first, the couple eventually made strong social connections and came to enjoy their new home. Now at midlife, the telling of this story gives them strength and hope that the new move will work out. Interestingly, they worried that story might be too "romantic," even as they wished for the current move to turn out as well [#030i].

Although couples shared war stories, they often were told with a sense of humor. Partners giggled at previous stupidities, made fun of their own misfortunes, laughed at their naiveté, and found comedy in the taxing absurdities they encountered at various times. The communication of humor has been implicated in resilience (DiCioccio, 2015). Some of these couples were experiencing acute adversity at the time of the interview, including health problems and financial difficulties. For them, expressions of humor seemed to release tension and free-up energy that might otherwise be wasted on worry or futile struggle. When recounting a series of disasters that had befallen them in recent years, Akira and Silas frequently dissolved in laughter. Even recent financial stressors were explained with levity. Akira says "it never costs to smile and laugh" [#15w]. By *sharing* in laughter they enacted a relational identity of hardiness, as a couple whose fun would not be spoiled by hardship. Indeed at least 10% of these couples described themselves as "crazy," "wacky," or "goofy" and a much larger group suggested that "have fun" was the best advice they could give to young couples. In short, as with war stories, funny stories helped couples cope with hard times. In the words of Mary Jane, they help "find happiness in this crazy world" [#87w].

Recalibrating Expectations: *"Marriage is not a fairy tale"*

For some couples, one way of dealing with life's disappointments was to adjust expectations, lowering them or making them more realistic. Recent challenges to his 23-year marriage to Tatiana, left Hector believing that "Marriage is not a fairy tale" [#269]. Partners described being humbled by the enormity of tragic events such as the death of a son or daughter. For others, chronic relational stress was attributed to unrealistic expectations regarding self, partner, or marriage. Jaden interviewed his parents Guy and Lindsey. Lindsey has been struggling a bit since Jaden, their youngest son, let for college. She is also realizing how her approach to life was affected by her parents' alcoholism. Lindsey has struggled with depression lately and the marriage has been challenged. The couple sought counseling, learning to "cut each other some slack." About his parent's midlife marriage, Jaden writes:

> ... one major change was being humble. In the earlier stages of their marriage, they were "high on life" with huge dreams about the way life was going to be. Over the years, they have become more accepting of the life they live, and realized that in fact it is a happier one than they had imagined. [128i]

Partners often described a struggle with perfection. Some realized that a spouse would never meet overinflated expectations as financial providers, sexual partners, roommates, or parents. Others looked inward. Lydia has come to realize that her struggle for the perfect marriage was a chronic source of stress—an exhausting and unrewarding waste of energy. What others might view as normal marital conflicts often escalated to crises in Lydia's mind, due to her own feelings of frustration and disappointment. Her husband Manuel made things worse by frequently describing Lydia as a "perfect" wife. Finally, she coped with the grind of unrealistic expectations by dialing them back and asking Manuel to drop the "perfect" language. Instead, he should say, "you are perfect ... *for me*." When things go wrong, Lydia no longer takes them so hard.

Re/discovering Assets: *"It really helps a person to realize what they have and to appreciate it"*

During times of strife, couples coped by drawing on relational assets. These were sometimes latent—sources of strength of which the couple was unaware of until a crisis struck. Other times, the couple rediscovered an asset which had been underappreciated or ignored. Natalie and Kirk moved to Colorado after the kids left home because they desperately needed a change. In career terms it was a "lateral move" for Natalie, but Kirk failed to find well-paid work. The couple were greatly disappointed in their new home, lonely and disoriented by the culture. It was then that they rediscovered their greatest asset: the family they had left behind. Although it had been her idea to move, Natalie missed the weekly gatherings with her siblings, children, and aunts. She had underestimated the importance of their advice, laughter, and emotional support during the recent hardship she and Kirk had endured. "Family is important" Kirk observed. "Family is *very* important" Natalie agreed. "When someone is used to one thing, then everything completely changes, it really helps a person to realize what they had and to appreciate it" [#78w,h].

The strength provided by extended family ties was referenced commonly in interviews, particularly when couples described coping with adversity. But other assets surfaced as well, some manifested in personal qualities attributed to a partner. Eve came to count on Guenther's ability to "stay cool" during a crisis [#195w]. And Aisha's experience as a nurse proved to be an asset when she and Jamar experienced a medical crisis [#141w,h]. "Calling in a favor" was one couple's way of describing their efforts to tap their social networks for job leads after a job loss [#178]. Yas and Nascha are members of the Navajo tribe who live off reservation. When Nascha unexpectedly lost her job during an economic downturn, the pair was strapped for cash. Her connections to the reservation proved to be an asset, as she would return there on weekends to make and sell traditional fried bread [043#]. This "sidelining"—having a secondary source of income—was observed to be a source of resilience in a study of families experiencing difficult economic times (Lucas & Buzzanell, 2012). In addition, Yas is known for his capacity to work hard; he "took on extra shifts" to help the family cope.

Finally, many couples spoke of their religious faith as an asset. Separate searches of the words "God" and "faith" suggest that as many 100 of these couples consider their faith a source of strength. I report on this in more detail below, under the heading *Finding a Higher Power*.

Forgiving and Reconciling: *"Getting back to a good place"*

Forgiveness is in part a process of acknowledging harmful behavior and foregoing one's right to recrimination and revenge. I discuss it here as a means of stabilizing relationships after a disruptive transgression. Communication scholar Sandra Metts has also written extensively about relational transgressions and the role that forgiveness might play in helping partners recover (e.g., Metts & Asbury, 2015). For current purposes it is enough to know that one motive for forgiveness is a desire to restore the relationship to an earlier state (Kelley, 1998). Indeed, one way partners communicate forgiveness is by allowing the relationship to "return to normal" (Waldron & Kelley, 2008). Forgiveness also makes an appearance in the next chapter where it is discussed as a source of relationship transformation rather than stabilization.

Pedro interviewed Rodrigo and Alma, his parents. The partnership has existed for nearly three decades, but they described painful midlife moments, some of which stemmed from Rodrigo's growing alcoholism. Pedro reported: "... forgiveness played a huge part in their relationship. Once they forgave each other, their relationship really started to change for the better. It went back to a good place. My parents are fighters and got through their battle" [#1291].

The path to reconciliation, or "getting back to a good place" often involves conditional forgiveness (Kloeber & Waldron, 2017). The aggrieved partner predicates forgiveness on compliance with requirements, such as "no more flirting at parties" or "check with me before spending more than 100 dollars." The conditions help manage the feelings of uncertainty and betrayal that serious transgressions trigger, and in that sense they help the couple cope with relational strife. In her interview, Jen confessed that it took years to rebuild trust after Will abused alcohol and consistently lied to her about the extent of his addiction. She found it "necessary" to forgive if they were to move on with their lives. But first he had to establish a track-record of sobriety [#191w].

Tatiana described a process of retuning a relationship that has experienced discord. For her forgiveness is:

> Coming into tune with what you're needs really are ... If you can't forgive, you cannot be in the relationship. It is not going to work. You have to be able to move forward. If you are constantly living in the back, or at the past, always looking at the prior situation and never feeling that there is never resolution, it will just get worse. [#269]

Escaping: *"The couple that does what they have to do but enjoys their karaoke time"*

Couples under stress described coping by escaping. "Taking a break," "grabbing some time together," "taking some time to clear our heads"—these and other phrases were used to describe the process. Dayna interviewed her parents, Lee and Ann, who have accepted the rather arduous task of providing nearly full-time care for three grandchildren. She wondered: How do they cope? As it turns out, they escape once a month to the local karaoke bar. They developed a fondness for that pastime in the 1990s, finding it a welcome distraction from the rigors of raising their four children. Dayna writes,

> When they do go out they have a list of requirements that have to be checked off before the night can be enjoyed. The grandchildren are placed with a babysitter

(myself). Then if all their "Ts" and "Is" are crossed and dotted, they are ready to hit the town. [#24i]

When asked how others would describe them, Lee offered this: "The couple that does what they have to do but enjoys their karaoke time."

Managing Boundaries: *"It was almost like having a third roommate"*

A fairly common coping approach involved creating clearer boundaries. In essence, couples described building barriers between them and the source of stress. This practice relieved them from unrelenting pressure or nagging annoyances that impinged on the relationship. Chronic stressors often involved ongoing friction with family members. With a boomerang child at home, couples might negotiate rules of privacy with the son or daughter. They specified parts of the home that were allocated for the exclusive use of the parties. Similar negotiations were had with parents who were under the care of the couple. Pedro observed his parent's efforts to manage their relationship with his older brother, who moved home after college. "At first there were some issues" Pedro observed, but his parents decided "our home is not a hotel." They kept their "guest" busy with chores but also granted him private space in their home [#129i]. Manny and Thelda were stressed by the chaotic return of their oldest child to the family home. Later when a second child retuned, they were ready with a clear set of rules. This time the experience was pleasant, according to Manny. "It was almost like having a third roommate. He had the same schedule as us, went to work, ate dinner, watched TV with us and went to bed" [#102h]. Rex and Wendy were less successful in managing boundaries with their son, who had trouble respecting house rules and brought undue drama to the household. "He had to go," Wendy reported in a voice choked by emotion.

Couples also described efforts to regulate their involvement with family members, including adult offspring who were now raising their own children. Lindsey, married to Guy for 30 years, advised: "You can't let the kids run the show, your mother-in-law interfere, or the job/career monopolize you. Balance and boundaries are key ingredients in the success of a marriage" [#128w]. The alternative was to "stick your nose where it doesn't belong" and suffer negative relational consequences. Other midlife pairs, distressed by what they considered to be the poor parenting or financial decision of offspring, imposed restrictions on their involvement in the financial affairs of sons or daughters. In another variation, couples discussed the limits of their involvement in the lives of their own parents. From the very beginnings of their marriage Briana's parents had discussed boundary setting. "Your grandparents had their own ideas about how to take care of children," her father noted. So the grandparents' interactions with the kids had to be monitored and regulated. Briana commenting on her parent's current boundary management efforts:

> Now that my grandparents are aging faster, my parents have started talking about boundaries with taking care of them. They are figuring out how much money they are able to give to their parents and if they are willing to let my grandfather move into our home. [#021]

In the interviews couples described efforts to limit discussion of troublesome topics, at least until a crisis had passed. For example, a spouse who was having trouble looking for a job might tire of a partner's frequent suggestions or critical comments. The resolution might be to limit, at least temporarily, marital discussions about job seeking while the spouse sought help from a career advisor or placement agency. Couples imposed other boundaries, such as banning current discussion of past transgressions or limiting the amount of time to be spent on gloomy topics. All of this boundary talk seemed designed to limit recurring or unnecessary stress as the couple allocated resources to shoring up the relationship and tackling midlife challenges.

Taking Time: *"Obviously it is not an overnight process"*

Advantaged by long experience, some midlife couples responded to crisis in a measured way, believing that the passing of time could in itself create conditions for positive change. For example, couples described letting time pass so anger could cool and hurt feelings heal. They repeatedly used phrases such as "a long time" to describe periods of recovery from transgressions or stressful events. "Taking one day at a time" helped couples feel less overwhelmed by trying circumstances. They often advised the young interviewers not to "rush" out of relationships when a challenge presented itself. One time-related coping practice involved delaying a response while the couple considered past experience, talked the situation over with friends, or weighed the current challenge in terms of the "bigger picture." In these ways, the passing of time broadened perspectives and helped couples develop flexible responses to the circumstances they faced. This kind of cognitive flexibility may facilitate resilience (Zautra, 2009).

Having persisted for many years, these couples often referenced "the long run" when they responded to momentary challenges. In the long run, they argued, unequal contributions balanced out, what was confusing became clear, painful conversations gave way to hard won understandings. Hanging in there for the long haul required "patience," a term invoked no less than fifty times in the interviews. After experiencing a hurtful affair and subsequent marriage counseling, Xianlin disclosed, "I feel it is finally changing us and making us even better than ever. Obviously it is not an overnight process but it does take time and patience. A LOT of patience" [#211w].

Direct Action

A smaller set of coping responses appeared to involve little communication. Instead they involved the taking of direct action by one or both partners.

Reallocating Work: *"Since that time, I knew that we could rely on each other"*

Relationship maintenance researchers have long argued that bonds are nurtured by a pattern of sharing work, such as child care or household tasks (e.g., Canary et al., 2002). Much of the relationship maintenance research has been conducted with less-experienced couples, but task sharing practices play a potentially important role in midlife resilience. In the current sample, the reallocation of work was often a temporary response, one that helped the partners cope during a challenging period. Often, pairs described reallocating domestic tasks in response to external stressors (e.g., a job loss) or to lighten the load of an overburdened partner. Han and and Ju are health professionals. He trained as a practitioner of traditional medicine and she as an M. D. Han's patient load began to decline as his specialty fell out of favor with clients. As a result Ju had to work longer hours to pay their expenses and Han was required to perform domestic tasks. As a traditional Chinese male he was uncomfortable having to "rely on" his wife's income, but Han somewhat grudgingly took on such duties as cooking and housecleaning during this period. In turn, Han remembers a time when he fell critically ill. His wife set aside all unnecessary commitments during that time, caring for her husband even as she ran her medical practice and managed the household. "Since that time," says Han "I knew that we could rely on each other."

Seeking Help: *"My father finally agreed to go to rehab and that was a huge turning point"*

Couples also coped by tapping community resources during times of stress or rapid change. Marriage counseling, faith communities, Alcoholics Anonymous, and other sources were mentioned. As Pedro left home and gradually entered adulthood, his father "slowly became an alcoholic," a fact his parents "kept secret" for several years. But his mother revealed during the interview that the marriage had become "extremely fragile" during this period. After two years of increasing relational distress, "My father finally agreed to go to rehab and that was a huge turning point." A partner's willingness to seek help was often interpreted as good sign, a necessary indication that he or she was committed to making things better. When offering advice to interviewers, some couples lamented waiting too long before seeking help. Others urged the students not to "go it alone" when trouble visited their own relationships. Indeed, a substantive minority of the couples had themselves sought marriage counseling, attended marriage retreats, or requested help from a pastor or faith community. In short, many of these experienced couples needed help, and they took action to locate it.

Re/Establishing Routines: *"We are the happiest we have ever been in our relationship"*

The resumption of routines was a final form of direct action. During times of crises partners insisted on resuming relational routines or creating new ones to make things as normal as possible. Although some of our couples were old enough and well-off enough to retire, leaving the workforce could be a disruptive relational experience. Carla was used to her own routines around the house. When husband Pat retired Carla grew irritable as she was unused to his constant presence. The couple had to make adjustments. They created new shared routines by signing up for tennis lessons and regularly attending concerts. Pat has rediscovered several latent hobbies and the couple travels together when the budget allows. After a rocky period, the couple is back on track. According to Carla, "We are the happiest we have ever been in our relationship" [#151w].

When Sam had a serious heart attack, the routines he shared with Audra were disrupted. No longer could they exercise together, dance, or travel. But as he slowly recovered, the pair adopted new routines to displace the unstructured and chaotic period when his life was at risk. The new normal in their relationship involves nightly walks around the neighborhood, hand in hand [#179]. Another couple described a similar experience. Cindy was diagnosed with breast cancer shortly after her last child left home for good. The diagnosis left her and Shawn feeling more appreciative of the time they have together.

Busy professionals, they started a new routine that would assure them couple time during the work week. Several days a week, Shawn and Cindy the leave their respective offices and meet for lunch [#059].

Taken together these practices replace uncertainty and disrupted relational patterns with predictability and ritualized behavior sequences. By sharing routines couples reaffirm their commitment during a time when it might be undermined by circumstances. By taking joint action, they exert control over circumstances rather than merely responding to them.

Root Metaphor Analysis

Table 5.2 lists metaphorical and figurative speech that we identified as these interviews were analyzed for evidence of coping practices. My purpose here is to supplement the descriptive but lengthy taxonomy of coping practices with

Table 5.2. Coping words and phrases.

Battle/war	Mediate; negotiate; talk it out
Bend	Normal; stable; routine; right the ship
Stand up; stand tall	Tuning, adjusting; tinkering
Bounce back	Dodging curve balls
Redemption/redeem/reclaim	Lighten up/lighten load
Investment; protect investment	Test; passing a test; trial
Conserving resources	Turn around; reverse course
Supporting/sustaining/encouraging	Revived ("revived her love"); on life support
Escape; change the scene	
Boundaries; off limits; create space	Healing
Give space; separate	Rediscovering; coming "full circle"
Flowing; go with flow; accept	Don't fall apart; keep it together
Draw closer; strengthen bonds	Toughen up; thick skin
The long run; long view; long time	Safe harbor; find safety
One step at a time; one foot in front of the other	Hash it out
	Deal with it (as opposed to avoid it)
Counting (your blessings; on family)	"Cards on the table"; bring to the table
Survive; endure; hang in; hold on	Anchor in the storm
Overnight ("It doesn't happen overnight")	Team; teamwork

a more parsimonious set of root metaphors. Ideally, these capture the primary dimensions of meaning used by these midlife couples as they made sense of the challenges they faced and the responses they enacted.

Based on word count alone, perhaps the most ubiquitous metaphor is *Relationship as a Battle*. Typically the couple "battled" outside forces, such as an economic downturn or ill health. Yet, sometimes they fought among themselves, as when they argued about the conditions under which an aging parent or boomerang child might live in their home. This metaphor highlights the intensity and high stakes of the challenges these couples faced. To win the war, they needed to "rally the troops" and draw deeply from their resources of courage, commitment, and family support. The practice of reestablishing solidarity flows from this war footing, as does the practice of managing boundaries. Partners joined forces and built barriers in their efforts to repel a threat. As do battle-tested soldiers, the couples reported strengthened relational bonds and they told stories which highlighted both struggle and triumph. When invoking this metaphor, couples seemed to be saying "we can survive anything, if we survived *this*." As suggested by Lucas and Buzzanell (2012) drawing upon these symbolic resources may promote resilience in the current moment even as it prepares the speaker for future battles. Seasoned by combat, couples seemed confident that they would prevail in the face of obstacles. In this sense the couples were enacting what Ouwehand et al. (2007) labelled *proactive* coping.

Another frequently-invoked metaphor was the *Relationship as Marathon*. Couples coped with adversity by focusing not on the short term but on the long run. It "takes time" they said and it doesn't happen "overnight." The relationship was a marathon, not a sprint, so couples needed to conserve resources, count on the support team, "hang in there," and endure. The coping practices that flow from this root metaphor include drawing on assets, taking time, and perhaps, recalibrating expectations (regarding one's abilities, the likelihood of short term rewards, or the presumed path to relational longevity). From this viewpoint, obstacles and roadblocks are to be expected, a certain amount of toughness and "thick skin" will be required, but with persistence and the passing of time the couple would prevail. This kind of sensemaking fosters hope by framing "midrace" challenges as the temporary discomfort that any distance runner would experience on the way to a rewarding finish. It may discourage couples from dropping out of the race too soon. Instead, they should dig deep, take one step at a time, and let time pass. Having already invested so much time, many of these couples were willing to take the long view.

A third prominent metaphor is *Relationship as Fine Tuning*. The focus here is on making adjustments in response to discord, stresses, or lapses in synchrony. It is expressed in such practices as honing communication skills, recalibrating expectations, reallocating work, and reworking routines. This approach highlights the need for adaptation, although these were often described as minor adjustments rather than radical reworkings. Coping was enacted by improving upon existing practices, accepting variations on familiar patterns, and rejecting rigidity. This way of thinking emphasizes interdependence and cooperation, as it typically involved adjustments by both partners. The system had to be by fine-tuned and partners brought into harmony so the relationship could prevail in the face of changing circumstances.

A fourth, but less pervasive, root metaphor I labelled *Relationship as "Dealing With It."* The metaphorical language flowing from this metaphor includes "hashing it out," "facing reality," "dealing with" the situation. In each case, these phrasings favor confrontation rather than avoidance of challenges. Sometimes that challenge came in the form of a partner who was overbearing, reckless, verbally abusive, or addicted to a substance. Several female spouses described relational turning points that featured them "standing tall" or "standing up" for themselves. Indeed, a subtheme is the importance of assertiveness and self-respect during times of martial conflict. "Dealing with it" often meant *talking* about it, making explicit what had been implicit or silenced. Partners expressed this preference with variations on the phrase "put your cards on the table." In this view resilient relationships are cultivated by courage, personal convictions, and a willingness to engage. This metaphor informed nearly all of the "communication intensive" adjustments and it can be seen clearly in the practice of forgiving and reconciling, which often involved an aggrieved partner making explicit the conditions that should be met if the partners were to reconcile.

Lesser Themes

Several other metaphorical threads were detected in the discourse of our interviewees. They each reveal a dimension of coping that is not fully captured by the metaphors described above. One of those could be labeled *Righting the Ship*. In addition to that phrase, participants invoked such terms as stabilize, return to normal, and anchoring. But rather than reveal how couples bounced back from adversity, these phrasings merely signified that they had done so. The root metaphors listed above were more suggestive of restorative action.

Nimbleness and/or *Light on Your Feet* were metaphorical terms implied by several participants who described "dodging curveballs," "lightening the load," or "reversing course." These phrases suggest that relational resilience involves flexibility and a willingness to change direction when faced with obstacles. Interestingly, this idea is central to nearly all resilience frameworks (Kent, Davis, & Reich (2013), but was rarely invoked by the couples we interviewed. One can argue as well that these nimbleness themes are implied by the more foundational metaphors described above. For example, reversing course may be a wise choice if one is lost during a marathon, a choice that might payoff in the long run.

Conclusions

In this chapter, I have described practices that appear to facilitate coping and the metaphors that couples use to describe their coping efforts. Perhaps the major contribution of this chapter is allowing couples to describe, in their own words, *how* they coped with the challenges of midlife. Of course, many other researchers have generated lists, sometimes truly exhaustive lists, of coping strategies (e.g., Skinner, Edge, Altman, & Sherwood, 2003). Others have simplified to a handful of approaches, such as emotion-focused or problem-focused. What may be unique here is my focus on the coping efforts described by couples, not just individual partners. And not just couples, but those who have long experience as couples. And of course, I have described their responses to the stresses of midlife, which, as we learned in Chapter 4 can be quite unique.

The results tell us quite a bit about the discourse that couples use as they enact coping efforts. In that way this study supplements recent research on the communicative enactment of resilience in families experiencing hard economic times (Lucas & Buzzanell, 2012). Indeed, the communication practices described by these couples demonstrate how they perform such functions as crafting normalcy. They appear to do it by creating new relational routines and by emphasizing solidarity in the face of potentially-divisive challenges.

Consistent with other recent resilience research (Socha & Torres, 2015), midlife couples coped by telling stories. War stories emboldened them in the face of adversity and funny stories made dark circumstances seem light. In this way couples engaged in the construction of "alternative logics" that facilitate resilience (cf., Lucas & Buzzanell, 2012). Consistent with a long line of research on the potentially ameliorative effects of cognitive reappraisal (Lazerus & Folkman, 1984), partners used humor to reframe adversity, to make it less ominous while reinforcing their identity as a hardy and even fear-less pair. Because they are middle-aged and experienced these couples actu-ally have stories to tell, and some of them were quite harrowing. The capac-ity to tell rich stories may be connected to emotional well-being at midlife (Lilgendahl & McAdams, 2011).

Previous work has suggested that redemption is a significant theme in sto-ries of midlife individuals as they confess to mistakes of the past and explain how they have made amends (McAdams, 2006; McAdams et al., 2001). The practice I identified as forgiving and reconciling serves a similar purpose at the relational level. Couples admitted to serious transgressions and recounted the steps they took to make things better. Forgiveness is a kind of emotion-focused coping (Worthington & Scherer, 2004). As such, it may have helped the couples persevere by replacing feelings of anger and despair with hope that things could be better. It appeared that a conditional approach to forgiveness ("I will forgive you if …") was a mechanism that facilitated coping. Often used when transgressions are severe, conditional forgiveness is a strategy for decreasing the likelihood that the transgression will reoccur (Kloeber & Waldron, 2017). It may assuage anxiety and anger and open the door to feel-ings of relief and benevolence. In turn, these positive emotions may allow partners to think more flexibly and creatively about the relational future (Metts & Asbury, 2015).

Another unique theme in this data involves the important role played by time. Couples used a rich vocabulary when talking about time. The passing of time was a marker of their resilience. In response to stress, they "took time" and sometimes merely let time pass until emotions cooled or circumstances got better. At midlife, couples still "had time" to make things better and, more than older couples, they could imagine a long relational trajectory. This prospect may have served as a motivator for change, as some couples seemed unwilling to spend additional years and decades dealing with unresolved rela-tional stressors. Hence some couples were inclined to "hash things out" now. Of course, they had also invested a great deal of time in their partnership, a factor that motivated efforts to cope rather than give up. At midlife, many couples adopted the long view, a perspective that made current challenges appear as temporary obstacles in a path that was likely to smooth out later.

Thus far I have discussed some of the ways in which this midlife sam-ple yielded unique insights. Of course, some of the findings are familiar. It is clear that a portion of coping practices were emotion-focused and others were problem-focused, two broadly familiar approaches for managing stress. Expressing assurances would be an example of the former and the "direct action" approaches are an example of the latter. However, it been suggested that these approaches vary in frequency and effectiveness, depending on such factors as gender, emotional competence, and whether the stressor relates to personal achievement or relational distress (Baker & Berenbaum, 2007). Because of the way we framed the questions for this study, nearly all stressors were described in terms of their relational implications and many of the relational practices could be classified as emotional coping. Yet, I would argue that this emotion-problem distinction obscures something important, the fact that many of these practices were *communication focused*. For long term couples facing midlife, it appears that re/focusing on communication is a prominent, and perhaps, effective coping approach.

In conclusion, I remind the reader that I reported in this chapter practices that normalized, stabilized, or restored relationships during times of adversity. As one interviewer reported after interviewing her parents, some of these relationships had "come full circle":

> Compared to the earlier years the couple feel like their relationship has come full circle. In the beginning the relationship was all about them and very intimate and after having kids that took a lot that away from them. Then after the kids grew up they feel like they have been able to go back to that romantic and intimate relationship they had when they were young. [#271i]

I have yet to explore practices associated with relationship transformation. Relational resilience includes coping, but it can also mean more. In Chapter 6, I listen for evidence of thriving and optimization. I report on couples who described relationships that grew after experiencing midlife challenges, seeking to identify practices and metaphors that facilitated not just restoration but reinvention.

References

Baker, J. P., & Berenbaum, H. (2007). Emotional approach and problem-focused coping: A comparison of potentially adaptive strategies. *Cognition and Emotion, 21*, 95–118. doi:10.1080/02699930600562276

Canary, D. J., Stafford, L., & Semic, B. A. (2002). A panel study of the association between maintenance strategies and relational characteristics. *Journal of Marriage and Family, 64*, 395–406.

Dicioccio. R. L. (2015). "We ould sure use a laugh: Buildin hope and resilience though humorous communication. In G. A. Beck & T. J. (Eds.), *Communicating hope and resilience across the lifespan* (pp. 34–52). New York, NY: Peter Lang.

Hoppmann, C. A., Gerstorf, D., Willis, S. L., & Schaie, K. W. (2011). Spousal interrelations in happiness in the *Seattle Longitudinal Study:* Considerable similarities in levels and change over time. *Developmental Psychology, 47,* 1–8.

Kelley, D. K. (1998). The communication of forgiveness. *Communication Studies, 49,* 255–271.

Kent, M., Davis, M. C., & Reich, J. W. (Eds.). (2013). *Handbook of resilience approaches to stress and trauma.* New York, NY: Routledge.

Kloeber, D. K., & Waldron, V. R. (2017). Expressing and suppressing conditional forgiveness in serious romantic relationships. In J. Samp (Ed.), *Communicating interpersonal conflict in close relationships: Contexts, challenges, and opportunities* (pp. 250–266). New York, NY: Routledge.

Lazarus, R. S., & Folkman, S. (1984). *Stress, appraisal and coping.* New York, NY: Springer.

Lilgendahl, J. P., & McAdams, D. P. (2011). Constructing stories of self-growth: How individual differences in patterns of autobiographical reasoning relate to well-being in midlife. *Journal of Personality, 79,* 2391–2428.

Lucas, K., & Buzzanell, P. M. (2012). Memorable messages of hard times: Constructing short- and long-term resiliencies through family communication. *Journal of Family Communication, 12,* 189–208. doi:10. 1080/15267431.2012.687196

McAdams, D. P. (2006). *The redemptive self: Stories Americans live by.* New York, NY: Oxford University Press.

McAdams, D. P. (2014). The life narrative at midlife. *New Directions for Child and Adolescent Development, 2014,* 57–69. doi:10.1002/cad.20067

McAdams, D. P., Reynolds, J., Lewis, M., Patten, A. H., & Bowman, P. J. (2001). When bad things turn good and good things turn bad: Sequences of redemption and contamination in life narrative and their relation to psychosocial adaptation in midlife adults and in students. *Personality and Social Psychology Bulletin, 27*(4), 474–485.

Metts, S., & Asbury, B. (2015). Unfolding the transgression scene. In G. A. Beck & T. J. (Eds.), *Communicating hope and resilience across the lifespan* (pp. 75–94). New York, NY: Peter Lang.

Ouwehand, C., de Ridder, D. T. D., & Bensing, J. M. (2007). A review of successful aging models: Proposing proactive coping as an important additional strategy. *Clinical Psychology Review, 27,* 873–884.

Skinner, E. A., Edge, K., Altman, J., & Sherwood, H. (2003). Searching for the structure of coping: A review and critique of category systems for classifying ways of coping. *Psychological Bulletin, 129,* 216–269. doi:10.1037/0033-2909.129.2.216

Socha, T. J., & Torres, A. (2015). Life's "war stories": Accounts of resilience and hope. In G. A. Beck & T. J. (Eds.), *Communicating hope and resilience across the lifespan* (pp. 219–234). New York, NY: Peter Lang.

Waldron, V., & Kelley, D. (2008). *Communicating forgiveness.* Newbury Park, CA: Sage.

Worthington, E. L., & Scherer, M. (2004). Forgiveness is an emotion-focused coping strategy that can reduce health risks and promote health resilience: Theory, review, and hypotheses. *Psychology & Health, 19,* 385–405.

Zautra, A. J. (2009). Resilience: One part recovery, two parts sustainability. *Journal of Personality, 77,* 1935–1943.

Zautra, A. J. (2013). Resilience is social, after all. In M. Kent, M. C. Davis, & J. W. Reich (Eds.), *Handbook of resilience approaches to stress and trauma.* New York, NY: Routledge.

· 6 ·

GROWING

This chapter is devoted to couples that reportedly grew stronger at midlife. After experiencing a substantive challenge of some kind, the partners reported that the relationship was different. And better. Increased intimacy, deeper understanding, improved satisfaction, better communication, more fun—these are among the quality improvements shared in our interviews. Optimization theories of aging emphasize that individuals may cultivate latent skills and talents as they gain wisdom, resources, and freedom from constraints imposed by self or society (Baltes & Baltes, 1990; for a review see Ouwehand, de Ridder, & Bensing, 2007). Moreover, some people report *growth* after experiencing adversity such as a severe illness or bad marriage (Tedeschi, Park, & Calhoun, 1998). In recent years resilience researchers have updated this line of work, providing evidence that adversity can spur growth at all stages of life, including middle age (Kent, Davis, & Reich, 2010). In this chapter, I look beyond the aging individual to the aging relationship, with a focus on the relational practices that seemed to foster not just coping, but thriving, in the face of adversity. To be included in this part of the analysis, couples needed to view the relationship as changed for the better, rather than simply normalized or stabilized. (This was established by examining responses to the interview question that asked couples to compare/contrast the marriage as it is now with the early years). I was guided by Zautra's view that resilience can be an optimizing response, one that it is intimately tied up in our social connections with others (2009, 2013). Evidence of growth often surfaces in the stories that middle-aged people tell about their aging (McAdams, 2006, 2014). For these reasons, I looked for evidence of thriving and growth in the stories couples told of their long relationships.

Of course, the line between growth and coping (the subject of Chapter 5) is sometimes fuzzy. These ideas share the connecting theme of adaptation. But, as I suggested in the last chapter, coping is more about making adjustments to existing practices, recalibrating the relationship without changing its essential elements. Coping involves bouncing back, returning to normal, but not so much a "new normal" or "bouncing forward." It certainly involves growth to some degree, but more often of the incremental kind. In contrast, relationship optimization may require something of a paradigm shift, a fundamental transformation of one or more dimensions of a long marriage. So I began by looking for practices that seemed transformational in that that they fostered or enacted deep relationship change. These are listed in Table 6.1. We will see that couples invented new ways to communicate, transformed or even reversed relational roles, dreamed about a new future, jettisoned plans as they responded to life-altering events (e.g., custodial grandparenting), radically altered their circle of supporters, and renegotiated the bases of relational power and respect. Some experienced relational transformation as a side effect of a consuming new passion, such as volunteerism, sport, or religious engagement. Some chose to terminate their relationship before later recoupling as two changed individuals committed to building a different kind of partnership.

In addition to delineating optimizing practices, I once again look at meaning making. What metaphors do these couples use to describe themselves to others? Our interview protocol explicitly requested that couples reflect on how their relationship has changed. That data proved particularly useful here as they revealed how relational identities might evolve in response to the passing of time and experiences of adversity. As discussed in Chapter 8, people naturally invoke metaphorical speech as they try to make sense of their relationships. My root metaphor analysis looks beyond answers to this particular interview question in an effort to identify a parsimonious set of core metaphors that are invoked by couples who seem to be thriving. Ultimately, this exercise yields insight about the symbolic resources that couples draw upon as they navigate the middle years of long relationships.

Before moving to the data, I must confess to being fascinated by processes of optimization. As I mentioned in Chapter 2, I have been somewhat obsessed

Table 6.1. Practices associated with growth and optimization.

Practice	Description
Communication-Intensive Adjustments	
Claiming respect	Asking for respect; renegotiating equality and fairness
Devising new roles	Expanding, reversing, modifying parts played by partners
Renegotiating autonomy	Granting or claiming more autonomy or togetherness
Expanding networks	Seeking new friends and perspectives; socializing differently
Family problem solving	Inviting the extended family to help address challenges
Dreaming together	Re/imagining possibilities; mapping a positive future
Reframing disappointment	Rethinking expectations; offering new rationales/logics
Forgiving and releasing	Taking responsibility; letting go of the past; pledging improvement
Enhancing intimacy	Self-disclosure; vulnerability; renewed sexual closeness
Investing in others	Creating a better future for grandchildren; volunteering, mentoring
Direct Actions	
Initiating new activity	Locating new hobbies and pastimes to be pursued jointly
Working differently	Adjust work to deal with adversity or improve relationship
Separating and rejoining	Living apart on a trial basis; divorcing and remarrying
Relocating	Changing geographic locations
Formalizing arrangements	Taking custody of grandchildren; marriage; seeking legal status

with creating an optimal marriage myself, not just settling for a run-of-the-mill one. As Kathleen might tell you, this search can be a little exhausting for her and for me. After all, the word "settling" has several connotations, including being comfortable with the choices you have made and not falling prey to unrealistic expectations, unproductive social comparisons, and utopian fairy tales. "Settling in," whether to read a good book or to live a good marriage, sounds pleasant indeed. So, the couples and practices in this section should not be perceived as practitioners of relational wizardry. They are not *better* than those featured earlier in the chapters on protective and coping practices. Rather, it is likely that couples negotiate the challenges of midlife in a variety of ways, some incremental and some more profound. For that reason, some couples make appearances in *each* of these chapters. In contrast, some partners found no reason to launch a major reworking of their marriage in response to midlife adversity. The relational tools and resources they had honed over the years proved handy in a time of crises. They were doing just fine, thank you. Others held on by their fingernails, coping long enough for the crisis to pass. But they *did* cope and things got better, often much better. But for the couples featured here in Chapter 6, coping appears to have been a necessary but not sufficient response to adversity. Let's see what they have to say.

Table 6.1 presents practices that were considered inventive and optimizing as opposed to protective or coping. As in Chapter 5, some of these midlife adaptations we labelled *communication-intensive* because in their accounts, couples emphasized crucial messages, talks, and negotiations. Most often, these changes were enacted *via* relational discourse. But, in some cases, it was the discourse itself that was targeted for change. For example, several spouses demanded more respectful communication from their partners. The communication itself had to change, they said, if they were to create a relationship that was more respectful, fair, and equal. Others changes we labeled *direct action* because they involved material practices, concrete steps designed to affect change in external circumstances. Some of these actions were mostly attributable to individual effort (e.g., seeking a new career) with apparently limited relational negotiation. However, another version involved coordinated action by the partners. In these cases, relational communication was implied, or was a likely consequence of the activity, but it wasn't a central element of the story. As an example, several couples took steps to acquire legal custody of grandchildren who were neglected by their dysfunctional parents.

Communication-Intensive Changes

Claiming Respect: *"We actually HEAR each other now"*

Some partners reported a flagging sense of self-regard at midlife, sometimes because their spouse now took them for granted or communicated in a disrespectful fashion. This feeling could be a powerful engine of relational change. Those who described it used forceful language, calling the behavior "totally unacceptable," "belittling," or "just wrong." The importance of the matter was conveyed in their nonverbal behavior: a lingering tone of resentment, an emphatic shake of the head, a voice quavering with disappointment or resentment. Kelley (2015) noted the importance of "justice talk" in interviews with long term romantic couples who had experienced serious transgressions. In the current sample, lack of respect was often cast as an injustice and a moral wrong. It sounded to us as if a basic relational right, the right to be treated as an equal, had been violated. The emotional potency of the violation, the reason the disrespected partner demanded deep relational change, was often found in the long history of the offensive behavior. Disrespected partners, and usually they were women, came to realize only at midlife that their contributions had long been devalued, that they were somehow "less equal."

In some cases, these discoveries were triggered by a particular event. A husband was observed to be openly flirting with a coworker at a party. A partner spent a large sum of money without consultation. But more likely the realization was gradual, a growing recognition that a partner used a mocking tone of voice in arguments, failed to take opinions seriously, valued his work over her work. The result was an "I-can't-take-this-anymore" call for fundamental change. What kinds of change?

Chris and Amy lived for many years with the relational fallout from his addiction to prescription drugs. She grew to disrespect him and by midlife their relationship was defined by a pattern of harsh arguments. Eventually he took steps to regain sobriety. The couple put their relationship on a new footing, a new commitment to "respect each other." Perhaps the most notable difference was a hard won capacity to be less reactive. "We actually HEAR each other now," Amy quipped. Comparing the past to the present, Chris reported: "We've 'lived life', [now] we appreciate and respect life" [#45w,h].

Some mistreated partners responded by overtly demanding equal treatment. Jeana's husband Allen was highly educated and used to winning arguments. When they disagreed he often used a condescending tone. At midlife Jeana realized that she was "fed up." After marriage counseling seemed to make little difference, Jeana announced that she was enrolling in a college located in a nearby city. She would return home on some weekends. Left to his own devices Allen realized that he had taken his spouse for granted. He began visiting Jeana on weekends. During their conversations Allen asked more questions and made fewer pronouncements. They talked about her classes and he read some of her assigned texts. The couple began to evolve what would come to feel like a more equal partnership.

Devising New Roles: *"I was no longer a part of it so I was upset"*

Partners also *devised new roles/identities*, a move that significantly altered their relationship and the parts played by each member. In some cases, new arrangements arose out of necessity and led to periods of discomfort and conflict. Bethany brought her boyfriend along when she interviewed parents Raul and Penny, who have been married 28 years. At midlife the couple negotiated a series of role changes.

> As their children moved out and they began separate careers, they began to work more as a team … equally sharing domestic duties at home. … When Penny decided to stop helping Raul with his wood flooring business and find her own career, Raul was supportive. She became a flight attendant, so they began to spend time apart more often than they had in the past. With her being away, Raul had to fill domestic roles around the house that he normally did not have to do. They described it as difficult at first, but eventually began new routines … They agreed that cleaning and cooking should be equal duties from that point on. "I would come home from my trips for work and he would have his new routine. I was no longer a part of it so I was upset and he was upset that I had been gone. So we talked about it and let each other know how we were feeling and it all worked out."

My student Rufus interviewed family friends Walter and Liz, who had been married 31 years. Due to Walter's illness they have made some adjustments. She went back to school and took on tasks that Walter used to perform. But he has learned to use the internet and his new role included finding them entertaining ways to spend time together.

> Walter was a very active person. He went motorcycle riding every weekend. But [due to cancer] he cannot do this anymore, and even sometimes he must sit on a wheelchair. It is very hard for Walter to adjust to this change. He lost part of his self-identity. Liz was also influenced by Walt's situation … She went back to the university to pursue a degree. This would be a turning point of their relationship. They rely on each other; they depend on each other. They collaborated in a new way. Liz spent more time with Walter after finishing school work and house-holding tasks. They watch television, get on blogs together. Their time when they are together makes their relationship closer. [#44i]

Renegotiating Autonomy: *"Getting to know each other again while getting to know ourselves"*

Some couples left the active parenting stage feeling too tightly bound together. For them, midlife meant loosening the ties that bind. They did this by mindfully granting themselves or their spouse time to explore latent or neglected interests. In some cases, this was uncomfortable for at least one partner who felt left out. But this discomfort was sometimes interpreted as a red flag, a sign that a relational identity defined by intense commitment was now smothering their identities as individuals. Despite some initial reservations, couples reported that these moves enriched their relationship. After decades of comfortable marriage Sam found that he and Audra needed more freedom. "Audra enjoys going out and shopping while I would rather stay home to take care of things around the house. We are getting to know each other again while getting to know ourselves" [#179h].

Julie had worked intensely all of her life and recently took early retirement. Her husband Scott recently bought a construction business and remains busy. Julie says she adjusted by learning to play golf. She also started a small business of her own. The couples are actually less busy than they were earlier in life and they spend more time together. But Julie finds that the relationship works better when their interests and days are not too intertwined.

Kelsey interviewed Randall and Macey, family friends and a "power couple." A second marriage for each, the partners' marriage has lasted 20 years. They recently took early retirement. However, despite their deep love and commitment they are now facing some challenges. Kelsey observed:

> They started a new real estate business; they never worked together before and are having some communication problems. He is used to having subordinates and wants to simply tell her what needs to be done. She is not used to being told what to do, having managed people most of her career. Macey said having hobbies and interests outside of the marriage was a great way to take a break from each other and do things separately. They love being with each other, but also like to be with friends sometime. They don't force each other to like and do everything together. She likes art museums and musicals, he does not really care for them. He likes football and hockey and she really don't care for them, so they agreed to go separately with like-minded friends. [#991]

Expanding Social Networks: *"Her circle of friends was somewhat limited"*

Couples also described *expanded socializing*, an intentional effort to enrich their social networks at midlife, to replace lost friends or keep their own conversations from going stale. In some cases previous friends had drifted away due to a loss of common circumstances such as raising young children. Inventive couples described expanding their social networks, a move that changed the dynamics of their relationship, typically for the better. Brianne interviewed her parents, who have been married 22 years. "Both of my parents grew up with traditional values," she reported. "Since she [mother] has not been in school or the workforce for about 21 years, her circle of friends was somewhat limited." But now in her mid-forties, her mom went back to college, and "enjoys meeting new people at school who have the same interests." This new set of friends has expanded the social opportunities for the couple. The expansion has caused some tensions as they rethink traditional ways of relating to themselves and others. "Communication is a struggle for my parents at this stage of their marriage."

For couples experiencing significant stressors, expanding the social circle seemed to help. They found new sources of advice, support, and fun. This seemed to relieve stress because the partners were no longer so reliant on each other. Ron and Gloria, in their 80s, were one of the older couples interviewed for this study. But in their interview with Josh, they recalled a period 20 years ago, when they retired, relocated, and became inventive in their efforts to find friends.

> So when they moved here they both realized they would begin spending all of their time together. It was a large adjustment for both of them, especially when Ron began having health problems that left him unable to drive. Ron states that the lack of independence was hard for him. Now not only was he not working "but had to rely on Gloria to chauffeur him around as well." So they both had to learn how to deal with each other. They said that what they found worked best was to go out and make new friends. Since they have so much time, they like to frequent restaurants and meet other regulars. [#118i]

Family Problem Solving: *"I appreciate my children more now than in the past"*

Some communication-intensive changes extended beyond the marital dyad to the larger social network, including the extended family. Most of our interviewees had managed their relationships in relative isolation, rarely calling on help for others. We saw some exceptions, particularly in Mexican-American families where extended family members were consulted about such matters as relocation or a new job. But even here the parents tended to be decision makers and other family members were primarily audience members who were simply informed about the intended course of action. At midlife some couples altered this practice, consulting more broadly and even taking direction from their children. For example, after supporting their children well into adulthood, one couple faced serious financial constraints after a job loss. Losing their house was a real possibility. In an unprecedented move they revealed the situation to their adult offspring and asked for help. A family meeting was convened. Drawing on the expertise of the kids, the couple devised a new financial plan. An older son volunteered to move home and start paying rent. This new dynamic of mutual aid has persisted. What is different is that the parents are now comfortable with both giving and receiving [#108i].

Ramon and Linda lost two of their six adult offspring in car accidents within one month. Devastated, the couple asked for help. The extended family responded by moving into the family home and helping with daily activities. The family is closer now and Ramon has come to appreciate that his remaining children have much to give the aging couple. "I appreciate my children more now than in the past; thanks to God, we have the opportunity to gather and see each other, because it can be the last time" [#84aH]. For others family problem solving was not borne of adversity. Instead it was simply a recognition that with maturation, their offspring now had much to offer in the form of expertise, understanding, and support—and a willingness to expand the circle of helpers.

Dreaming Together: *"A happy wife means a happy life"*

Thelda always wanted to own a toy shop. She and her husband Manny imagined a future in which they would work together to make that happen. At midlife, Manny encouraged her to pursue the dream and arranged his own life to help make it happen. He curtailed his own work hours, held down the domestic side of the house, and pitched in to help with the shop as needed. He encouraged his wife to travel to conferences and supported her through economic downturns. Indeed, collective dreaming was a practice engaged in by some couples. For them, dreaming was an essential part of their relational identity ("We have always been big dreamers"). For some talking about new and improved prospects was a way to direct attention away from current stresses while constructing a hopeful path to the relational future. In Manny's case, supporting Thelda's dream assured him that their future would be pleasant. "A happy wife means a happy life," he smiled [#102h].

Reframing Disappointment: *"They now see it as a blessing"*

When faced with disappointment, optimizing couples changed their criteria for defining a successful relationship. The opposite of rigid persistence, this approach involved a mutual effort by the partners to redefine what they wanted from life and from other people. Humility, often hard won, was evident in their discourse, as was flexibility. Some couples had learned to use what Lucas and Buzzanell (2012) called "alternate" logics, entertaining new rationales to explain how things had gone wrong and how they could be made right in the future. As one illustration, consider that Lupe's parents went from "failed" to "blessed."

> … my sister who was their "baby" got pregnant, and it shattered their world. They didn't know how to cope with it; they felt they had failed as parents. Their dream for us was to walk out of our house dressed in white the day of our wedding, and now that dream wouldn't come true. My parents were extremely disappointed; they wouldn't talk to my sister and were forcing her to marry the guy. However, once my nephew was born, it completely changed their world and they now see it as a blessing. This baby brought a new joy to my parent's lives; they love the role of being traditional grandparents. … They feel that this baby has given them a new light, since their kids are grown this baby is able to fill that void and give them something to look forward to. [#74i]

Forgiving and Releasing: *"Forgiveness was hard when I felt like he didn't respect me"*

While acknowledging that forgiveness is in part a psychological process, in our previous work Doug Kelley and I defined forgiveness as a *relational* process, one largely driven by the communicative acts of the parties.

> Forgiveness is a relational process whereby harmful conduct is acknowledged by one or both partners; the harmed partner extends underserved mercy to the perceived transgressor; one or both partners experience a transformation from negative to positive states, and the meaning of the relationship is renegotiated with the possibility of reconciliation. (Waldron & Kelley, 2008, p. 5)

As we saw in Chapter 3, the memory of long-ago transgressions can linger into midlife, a time when couples may find the motivation and the emotional resources to deal with them. The erosive effects of blame can make the relationship brittle and midlife couples may feel the need to finally "clear the air" and "move past" hard feelings. A couple's approach to forgiving predicts improvement in relational quality (Kelley & Waldron, 2005), as confirmed in our interviews with very long term romantic couples (together 40 years on average).

In Chapter 5 we discussed conditional forgiveness as a coping strategy. Harmed partners sought to reestablish relational stability and predictability by requiring compliance with certain rules ("always call home if you will be late";

"no drinking with your buddies after work"). Typically these were relational standards that the aggrieved party *assumed* were in place prior to the transgression. In this way forgiveness was a process of reasserting relational expectations and returning the relationship to normal after a period of disruption. For these couples forgiveness offers a path to reconciliation. In this chapter I feature couples who described forgiveness as a transformative process, one that created substantial, permanent, and positive relational growth. It was also a process of releasing the relationship from the past so it could grow into the future.

Shane and Dawn gave an example of the connection between forgiveness and relational growth. We see that forgiveness "was hard" until they developed mutual respect. But they learned to forgive as they grew "together and separately."

> A major challenge was learning to manage our money. We would both spend frivolously without consulting the other. Each time either of us did this it hurt the other one deeply. The worst was when he came with a brand new car when I had just taken a salary cut at work. I was furious! We had to learn to forgive each other for these things and it allowed us to grow together and separately as better financial handlers. Luckily, the car was returnable, and after a few months we got a nice used car with only 14,000 miles on it, and we saved $16,000. We conquered the goal by creating a budget and following it. Communicating with each other and really making sacrifices. Forgiveness was hard when I felt like he didn't respect me enough to ask my opinion on things. [#102w]

This linking of forgiveness and growth was not unusual. Raj became a stepfather to Margaret's two kids and the couple added several of their own. Over the years resentment built between the pair as they disagreed on parenting, schooling, and coordinating with the biological father. Raj's stepchildren blamed him for the loss of their father. Through all of this, the couple wanted to maintain a relationship that made their family feel genuine and "real," like a "team." Margaret sees forgiveness as the process, albeit an imperfect one, that allowed old wounds to heal and genuine relationships to form.

> I think every couple goes through this process or learning to forgive and in some cases forgive and forget. I will be quite frank with you. We aren't perfect, but what couple is perfect? We have had our ups and downs but like Raj said, "We are a team." We work together through each of our differences and over time we have learned to talk through our problems. [#28w]

Many other couples credited forgiveness when discussing relational growth. They learned not to "hold grudges," to "let go" of blame, and to "put the past in the past"—all of which helped their relationship mature, enhanced their communication, and freed them to focus on the future.

Enhancing Intimacy: *"This has … made them fall more in love with each other"*

Optimizing couples described efforts to enhance their closeness, both emotional and physical. Midlife offered new freedom to explore their sexuality and deepen feelings of love. After interviewing her parents Lupe wrote:

> Now that my sister and I are on our own, my parents have been recoupling. They started having date nights, about 3 days out of the week. They will either go out for dinner together and/or movies. It's been like this for about the last couple of years. They'll pick random nights to go out for walks to the park, just them two. I feel that this has helped them rekindle their love and has made them fall more in love with each other. [#74i]

After Chuck (at the age of 52) suffered two heart attacks in six months, his sex life suffered. His wife Marilyn began to feel distant. In the interview she even admitted that she considered leaving Chuck and he confirmed that the couple nearly separated. However, they both committed to seeing marriage counselors in a bid to save the marriage. The counseling helped the couple to think more innovatively about their sexual relationship. Although reluctant to share details, Chuck and Marilyn explained that a counselor helped "giving them alternative ways to please one another without actually having sex" [#006i]. Having survived this period of diminished intimacy, the couple reported, is one reason the relationship is stronger than ever.

Investing in Others: *"She was willing to allow me to learn from her experience"*

At midlife, many of our couples turned their attention outward, joining together in an effort to help others learn from their own experiences. Indeed, participating in these interviews was one example of *generativity*, a concern for future generations (McAdams & Guo, 2015; McAdams & Logan, 2004). Generativity took a variety of forms, but to be included here, the generative activity had to be both shared by the couple and integral to their evolving relational identity. It had to be something they viewed as part of their relational narrative. Many couples explained to student interviewers that they were sharing "lessons learned," some "hard earned" advice to help the students "avoid the mistakes we made." Shonda was grateful to her interviewee (Amy), for "sharing some intimate things with me about a hard time in her life [her husband's addiction] and I am grateful that she was willing to allow me to learn from her experience and knowledge" [#45]. Her comments were echoed by many other student interviewers.

Couples with children often talked about their concern for future generations. Some delighted in the transition to being a grandparent couple and frequently pitched in to help their offspring raise them. In some cases, the shared cause of grandparenting offered relational salvation. Eduardo reported about the couple he interviewed.

> Catalina specifically states that grandchildren were a primary factor in wanting to sustain their relationship and seeking to improve their interactions. Having grandchildren gave them both a different perspective on relationships. It brought them to experience a new aspect of life, taking an active part in helping to raise their own grandchildren. [#67i]

But other couples simply expressed a desire to "give back." They did so by offering marriage preparation programs at their churches, coaching youth sports, offering support to young parents in their neighborhoods, and numerous other intergenerational investments.

Direct Action

Although it would be hard for any relationship adjustment to be undertaken without communication, couples did describe material practices that helped them respond to adversity. In these cases, it was taking individual or collective action that couples most emphasized in their interviews. As with the communication-intensive practices partners associated these actions with relationship transformation, not merely reestablishing equilibrium. Given that my primary interest lies with the discourse that makes couples resilient, I will describe these actions only briefly. They are also described in Table 6.1.

Initiating Shared Activity: *"Like those high school kids who fell in love all over again"*

Some couples reinvented their relationships by *doing*. They described new activities that substantially changed their relationship for the better at midlife and beyond. These joint pursuits injected novelty, became the foundation for new rituals, allowed them to interact with new groups, and placed the partners in the presence of unfamiliar people. New activities can bring spontaneity back to a relationship that has become routinized or dull (Waldron & Kelley, 2009). But more than that, our couples described a refined relational identity, a different sense of who they were and how they would be described by others. Among the new midlife activities were travel, dance lessons, bicycling, hiking, theater and a host of other joint endeavors.

One of the biggest changes and challenges faced by Jin and Xianlin has been the absence of their adult offspring. But, as he observed, they are working together to fill that gap in their lives:

> Not having the kids 24/7 will be an opportunity for growth. We are learning how to deal with some things, like what we can do together and mesh our interest. Perfect example: I like stupid funny movies or some with action and she doesn't, so for us to go to the movies is a big dilemma. Someone is giving into something one way or another. Before it was what the kids wanted to see, now it's got to be a give-and-take compromise. [#211h]

Brent and Lauren's shared activity (hunting) was unusual in our data, but the way it transformed their relationship was instructive and fairly typical. Here is what they told Stephen, the son of a friend.

> … it was not until late 2004 that Brent had finally recovered from cancer and grew out of his depression. … With health on their side, they chose to revitalize their love for one another by pouring their energy into a new activity that neither one of them had experienced before, hunting. … After a few casual hunts with friends, they "heavily invested" into their own camping and hunting gear and spent most of their weekends in the woods together. They grew excited for each weekend that they spent together and part of their fun was also deciding what animal hunting "applications" they wanted to choose together. From 2005 to 2012 they planned, bought, camped, enjoyed and hunted very frequently and before they knew it, they "were like those high school kids who fell in love all over again." [#123i]

Working Differently

The category working differently includes career-related actions taken by one or both spouses. To be included here the action must have been a response to acute or chronic adversity. And, the couple must have perceived the action as one that transformed the relationship in positive ways. Felipe and Josephina, married twenty-nine years, provided one of many examples. Faced with an empty nest, Josephina describes herself as "out of a job" and feeling lonely. For years Felipe's work with the railroad kept him away from home for long stretches of time. But recently, in an effort to be closer to his wife, Felipe started his own insurance business. Josephina says she "appreciates" her husband's efforts to bring them closer both geographically and emotionally [#290]. Other couples described starting new businesses together, coordinating their off days to make time for shared hobbies and activities, or seeking new jobs that would be more relationship-friendly.

Separating and Rejoining

For a handful of these couples temporary separation was another form of direct action. Locked in dysfunctional patterns of communication or simply bored with the long relationship, these couples decided to live apart, at least for a trial period. Having reflected and changed, the partners rejoined and the relationship bloomed as one couple said, "better than ever." For these partners, the intentional decision to recommit is now an important part of their relationship narrative, a reminder of how the bond shouldn't be taken for granted. As told to their daughter Leila, the story of Sean and Angie represented a rare case (in our sample) of verbal abuse, followed by separation. Angie shared these words while Sean was out of the room:

> I tried to leave once. … I was gone for four months. You kids had left, I had nothing to do, no one and your father just wanted to tear at me. I just wanted to go. So I did. Getting old is not for the faint of heart—you have such great life changes and sometimes it's hard to deal with. … We hadn't had sex in nearly 20 years. When I came back to him, it was like we were newlyweds again.

Relocating

Relocation was identified in Chapter 4 as a kind of adversity that challenged many couples. But for some, moving was a strategy intended to help the relationship thrive. Couples put distance between themselves and difficult family members. Some left behind business failures, expensive cities, or poor climates intending to "turn over a new leaf" or seek a fresh start. In the cases included here, the move was narrated as a boon to the relationship, a reason the couple is thriving now. But that doesn't mean the relocation was easy. "I had to leave all of my friends, my job, my church and start over in a city where we didn't know anyone" [#183i]. That was Teresa describing the move that she and Gene made some years earlier. They moved because of Gene's job and improved economic prospects. But looking back, Teresa thinks the experience proved she and Gene were open to change and willing take a chance—characteristics that seem to define this couple now, at midlife. Because they had no family of friends nearby, the partners depended on each other. The relocation drew them closer then and the memory seems to keep them close now.

Formalizing Arrangements

A small but still noteworthy number of couples described formalizing relational arrangements as a way to optimize a relationship that was subject to present or future adversity. Grandparents sought custody of grandchildren to protect their shared status as guardians. Gay couples consulted attorney's about protecting their assets and assuring that their partner could exercise the rights that (until recently) were denied gay couples. Long-time partners finally decided to marry as a sign of their commitment and, sometimes, due to such necessities as employer-sponsored health insurance. Couples clarified their inheritance policies and updated retirement plans to affirm to all that their relationship has a couple was prioritized over previous marriages and various family relationships.

It is worth noting that formalizing was sometimes interpreted as a relationally problematic action. For grandparents, a request for custody could deeply strain the couple's relationship with the grandchild's parents, their own offspring. Russ and Dwayne viewed formal marriage with skepticism. A same-sex couple of 20 years, they chose *not* to marry, even though recently it had become legal to do so. They reject the hetero-normative idea that marriage is necessary to legitimate their bond and they described seeing married but apparently unloving cross-sex couples sitting silently in restaurants. Views of legal marriage are changing they observed, and not just their own. Dwayne said it this way: "People today are more open to different views, and they used to consider marriage between a man and a woman. But today they just view it as love no matter what gender they are" [#86].

Root Metaphor Analysis

As noted in Chapter 8, a root metaphor is a basic conceptual framework upon which meanings are layered. Here, as in Chapter 5, I consider how interviewees made sense of their midlife relationships, cognizant that the metaphors of growth and optimization have been shaping my own interpretations.

Table 6.2 provides a list of metaphorical phrases used by optimizing couples. The first step in the analysis was simply to list as many metaphors as

Table 6.2. Relationship growth words and phrases.

Energy transfer	Delight
Re/invigorated: "The fountain of youth"	Soul mates
Redefined, reimagined	Confessing; "owning up"
Discovery/insight/enlightenment	Reengaged ("2nd honeymoon"); "actively dating"
Exploration; adapting to a "new world"	Expanding the pie
Dreaming/imagining	Recruiting family members;
Spinning out (a new future)	Role reversal ("now *they* give us advice").
"What doesn't kill you makes you stronger"	"Making up for the past"
	"Coming clean"
Ann found out "the hard way"	"A new life together"
Making (new) plans; "game planning"	"A turning point for us"; watershed moment
"The person she was becoming"	
Invention/reinvention/reimagining/ Rethinking (self and other)	"Big deals"
	Stronger bonds
"Lessons learned"	Catalyst for change
Imperfection; humans make mistakes	Solving a puzzle; figuring it out
Negotiating	Finding "the directions"
Enriching	Barn building (need help from others)
Truth telling	Reach out (seek consultation)

possible. From there I analyzed the sets of exemplars, looking for similarities and differences in meaning. As groupings emerged, I tried to identify those that expressed or qualified a deeper, foundational concept. Those deeper concepts were identified as root metaphors.

Relationship as Adventure

A number of these expressions tap the theme of *Relationship as a Journey*, a coping metaphor I explored in Chapter 5. The difference here is that the journey is rarely described as arduous. Rather these couples describe traveling together as an adventure, one marked by exploration, risk, discovery, and new insights.

Closely aligned to this metaphor are the ideas of dreaming and imagining, and also planning together, as couples appear to grow in the process of mapping a fulfilling and exciting future. Other related themes include "finding the directions" to a good relationship and to a lesser extent "solving the puzzle," which seems to suggest finally finding one's way through a maze of clues The idea of "soul mates" was mentioned several times. One could describe these partners as kindred spirits, fellow travelers on a path of enriching adventure.

Relationship as Growth

Relationship as Growth is another fundamental theme. We see this expressed in both individual ("the person she was becoming") and relational ("a turning point for us") terms. Some couples described a kind of metamorphosis as they matured, freed themselves from unhealthy patterns of relating, and came closer to their potential. Growth was also equated with "lessons learned," sometimes the "hard way." The clichéd expression, "what doesn't kill you makes you stronger" also seems to fit here, as does "rethinking" the relationship, "redefining" it, and growing into changed relational arrangements ("role reversals").

Relationship as Redemption

The root metaphor of redemption was less commonly expressed, but it did take several forms. Some couples referenced the importance of confessing past misdeeds, telling the truth, coming clean, and making up for the past. Having resolved to put hurt behind them, these couples "found new life" together. For some that involved an exciting reboot of the relationship, "dating all over again" or "a second honeymoon" or "renewing our relationship."

Lesser Themes

Less prominent but still quite descriptive were the metaphors related to energy transfer, enrichment, and building bonds. The first of these was exemplified by a mother who described pleasure at being able to transfer her energy from parenting to career and relationship projects. The second seemed to draw on a mining-the-resource metaphor, suggesting that midlife was a period of unearthing latent capacities and tapping new reserves of strength. The third was more common as partners described the development of new and/or stronger connections between themselves, with family members, and with friends. For some these bonds were forged in the fires of shared adversity. For others, it was a midlife decision to invest more time and energy in relationships that left them feeling more firmly connected to others and to each other.

Conclusions

The data presented in this chapter suggest some differences in the symbolic practices that facilitate the thriving, coping, and protecting dimensions of relational resilience. In contrast to most protective factors, optimizing practices appeared to be *uniquely crafted* to meet changing conditions or a midlife challenge. In that way, they *emerged* from conditions encountered along the lifecourse. They are not "off the shelf" responses, deployments of well-used relational tools, blue prints for relational success. Rather, they are *inventive* practices though which couples enact a relationship that is in some significant way novel and different, one predicated on the root metaphor of adventure. These couples came to see change as necessary, inevitable, and potentially exciting. These optimizing couples described rethinking, reinventing, and reimagining. Indeed, those who invoked the adventure metaphor seemed to value open-endedness, contingency thinking, and the future. Their accounts downplayed such relational qualities as predictability, preparedness, present-focus, and adherence to routines and roles. Brent said it this way:

> But everything is still exciting. Our life is still an adventure. I wake up feeling more accomplished than any other aspect of my life by looking at my wife and reflecting on what we have been through together. I look forward to whatever else life may bring us. But I'm not the same youngster who thinks that every aspect of our (marital) adventure is going to be positive. What's changed in our marriage is our perspective on life through our reflection of the past.

The metaphor of relational growth highlights processes of mutual learning and maturing. It positions challenges and adversity as opportunities for learning. Couples sometimes described a kind of trial-and-error process that unfolded over extended periods of time and repeated rounds of communication as they made sense of a changing situation or ambivalent feelings. For example, one couple described a lengthy and mindful effort to evolve a "new kind of relationship" with an adult son who continually asked for financial support. They bandied about metaphors that might be more useful than "parents," "bankers" or the even more distressing "enablers." Mentors? Guides? Boosters? The metaphor of growth positions relational success as a matter of developed wisdom, some of which is earned and some which is cultivated from free thinking dialogue. It devalues "received wisdom" and, as with the adventure metaphor, leads to anxiety about relationships that have become too stable or even dull. In this sense it is different from the metaphors of coping which emphasize steadying, stabilizing and normalizing during times of turbulence.

The redemption metaphor emphasizes that problems of the past needn't proscribe the future. It suggests that individual partners, and the couple, can "earn back" such relational goods as trust and intimacy. But, redemption requires change and a mutual commitment to a future that looks different and better (for an interesting discussion of redemption in life narratives see McAdams, Reynolds, Lewis, Patten, & Bowman, 2001). Redemption is connected to the restoration of mutual respect and relational justice. By using this metaphor couples seem to embrace hope while rejecting discourses of blame and despair. From this viewpoint even serious moral mistakes are rejected as grounds for relationship termination. Instead, couples appear to accept imperfection and strive to "refine" or "remake" themselves and their relationships.

The familiar adage "necessity is the mother of invention" certainly applies here as adversity was the catalyst for these learning and redemptive responses. In some cases change was initiated by one of the partners determined to make the relationship more satisfying and responsive to new realities. For example, one spouse's extreme dissatisfaction with her post-parenting role prompted her to initiate very pointed discussions about her desire to return to college and the relational rethinking that would entail for both partners. In other cases a desire for radical change appeared to be mutual from the very beginning, often because the partners were simultaneously affected by a stressful event, such as the sudden illness of a parent or the misfortunes of their offspring.

In conclusion, let me offer that some of the findings in this chapter were expected based on previous research. One of these was the role of *forgiveness*, which has previously been identified as a component of relationship longevity (Waldron & Kelley, 2008, 2009). Some midlife couples nurture grudges over earlier incidents such as acts of infidelity, autocratic decision-making or financial recklessness. At midlife some of these incidents "come home to roost" or "come to a boil." Our couples reported efforts to "stop blaming" or discuss calmly issues that previously left them, as one participant described it, "screaming and yelling." For some, adopting a more forgiving approach was an ongoing challenge: "a big learning lesson for the umpteenth time." Forgiveness involves both recognition of harm and a commitment to be merciful, a willingness to let go of bitterness and the understandable desire for retribution. Our data suggest that forgiveness was prominent in the relational narratives of some thriving couples. It is one expression of the root metaphor of redemption.

However, a number of communication practices described by couples were not fully anticipated by my reading of previous literature. Some of these emerged due to the unique challenges and opportunities of midlife. One of these was family problem solving, a collective approach that is sometimes forced by the vicissitudes and dependencies of very old age. But at midlife couples are typically capable of autonomous decision-making and they tend to function primarily as a dyadic unit. In contrast to expectation, some of our midlife couples *chose* to expand decision-making conversations to include adult children and members of the extended family. Some couples found that making major decisions in isolation was no longer effective. Some realized that adult offspring now have greater capacity to offer resources such as financial help, wisdom, and emotional support. We saw this with couples who "rallied the troops" to share the load of looking after their own aging parents. This proactive seeking of resources may be a marker of relational thriving. Perhaps couples who "go it alone" at midlife experience more stress, conflict, and exhaustion.

In general, what we saw here were inventive practices born of necessity, commitment, creativity, or some combination thereof. And I would be remiss if I failed to mention the sheer tenacity of some of these couples, who persisted despite the sometimes harrowing circumstances described in the third chapter of this book. As I read their accounts I really could *not* conclude that they clung together out of desperation or a lack of alternatives. Rather, I think they brought a sense of imagination to the relationship, a shared sense of adventure, and yes, a certain tenacity. In describing his long partnership with Joyce, Al captured nicely my own impression.

It took us a long time to get to this point in our relationship. We experienced it all from financial woes to family misunderstandings. But we love each other now more than ever. Because we believe we have something special and we will not let it go.

References

Baltes, P. B., & Baltes, M. M. (1990). Psychological perspectives on successful aging: The model of selective optimization with compensation. In P. B. Baltes & M. M. Baltes (Eds.),

Successful aging: Perspectives from the behavioral sciences (pp. 1–34). New York, NY: Cambridge University Press.

Kelley, D. K. (2015). Chapter 4: Just relationships. In V. R. Waldron & D. K. Kelley (Eds.), *Moral talk across the lifespan: Creating good relationships* (pp. 75–94). New York, NY: Peter Lang.

Kelley, D. & Waldron, V. (2005). An investigation of forgiveness-seeking communication and relational outcomes. *Communication Quarterly, 53,* 339–358.

Kent, M., Davis, M. C., & Reich, J. W. (Eds.). (2010). *Handbook of resilience approaches to stress and trauma.* New York, NY: Routledge.

Lucas, K., & Buzzanell, P. M. (2012). Memorable messages of hard times: Constructing short- and long-term resiliencies through family communication. *Journal of Family Communication, 12,* 189–208. doi:10.1080/15267431.2012.687196

McAdams, D. P. (2006). *The redemptive self: Stories Americans live by.* New York, NY: Oxford University Press.

McAdams, D. P. (2014). The life narrative at midlife. *New Directions for Child and Adolescent Development, 2014,* 57–69. doi:10.1002/cad.20067

McAdams, D. P., & Guo, J. (2015). Narrating the generative life. *Psychological Science, 26,* 475–483. doi:http://dx.doi.org/10.1177/0956797614568318

McAdams, D. P., & Logan, R. L. (2004). What is generativity? In E. de St. Aubin, D. P. McAdams, & Tae-Chang Kim (Eds.), *The generative society: Caring for future generations* (pp. 15–31). Washington, DC: American Psychological Association.

McAdams, D. P., Reynolds, J., Lewis, M., Patten, A. H., & Bowman, P. J. (2001). When bad things turn good and good things turn bad: Sequences of redemption and contamination in life narrative and their relation to psychosocial adaptation in midlife adults and in students. *Personality and Social Psychology Bulletin, 27*(4), 474–485.

Ouwehand, C., de Ridder, D. T. D., & Bensing, J. M. (2007). A review of successful aging models: Proposing proactive coping as an important additional strategy. *Clinical Psychology Review, 27,* 873–884.

Tedeschi, R. G., Park, C. L., & Calhoun, L. G. (1998). *Posttraumatic growth: Positive changes in the aftermath of crisis.* Mahwah, NJ: Erlbaum.

Waldron, V., & Kelley, D. (2008). *Communicating forgiveness.* Newbury Park, CA: Sage.

Waldron, V., & Kelley, D. (2009). *Marriage at midlife: Analytical tools and counseling strategies.* New York, NY: Springer.

Zautra, A. J. (2009). Resilience: One part recovery, two parts sustainability. *Journal of Personality, 77,* 1935–1943.

Zautra, A. J. (2013). Resilience is social, after all. In M. Kent, M. C. Davis, & J. W. Reich (Eds.), *Handbook of resilience approaches to stress and trauma.* New York, NY: Routledge.

SECTION III

THEORY, METHODS, AND MEASURES

· 7 ·

THEORIZING RELATIONAL
RESILIENCE AT MIDLIFE

Gary A. Beck (Old Dominion University)

On September 24th, 1969, Erik Erikson lectured a group of students and faculty at Harvard on the topic "Landing on the Moon" (Schlein, 1989). In it Erikson detailed conversations he held with older men about their impressions of one of the most important scientific events of that era, Neil Armstrong's landing and walking on the moon. Erikson revealed a telling quote to that audience, with one interviewee suggesting that moonwalk was possible because "the kingdom has always been within each of us, if we can only learn to face it—and to share it." Life's broader and more profound questions have to do with the meaning or purpose for our tireless day-to-day efforts, the reason for larger more impactful events, as immensely challenging and defeating or as uplifting and largely rewarding they may be. Erikson's quote speaks to the potential for either, and the power we each have in building bridges or breaking down barriers for future generations. In essence this reflection suggests our potential to generatively work together and strive for great heights (e.g., the moon); this is only possible by moving generations forward practically and by iteratively advancing knowledge and innovation.

This quote captures an often-understated essence and profound potential impact of those in middle-age. Within the larger framework of interdisciplinary and communication scholarship, especially that oriented toward lifespan, midlife investigations can feel like the "last uncharted territory" of the life course (Brim, Ryff, & Kessler, 2004, p. 1). This honor is in part due to the historical overemphasis on child development (Masten & Wright, 2010), as well as the necessity of generally more complex methodological choices and less *convenient* sampling (Pitts & Hummert, 2014). In other words, investigations into the lives of midlife adults are more challenging than those of college students.

The investigation reported in this volume has been born in part out of the desire to better represent the breadth of the human experience across the lifespan. For example, relationships and careers naturally have trajectories (see Huston, Surra, Fitzgerald, & Cate, 1981), children become adults through the combination of daily incremental growth and formative moments (Baltes, 1997; Erikson, 1950; Lerner, Jacobs, & Wertlieb, 2005) and our experiences with natural disasters and our ecological circumstances unfold over time (Gunderson, 2000; Longstaff, 2005; Merolla, 2015). As it relates to this volume, those in midlife (typically ages 40–60, or 65) experience unique incremental and acute moments of transformation, bereft with new challenges and opportunities, only to respond with the "ordinary magic" of resilience (Masten, 2001).

Culturally, midlife is an age period seemingly viewed with an interesting combination of ambivalence, amusement, and contempt. Both men and women alike bemoan being "over the hill," leading some to obscure their age to both themselves and others as result. To these defiant people "age is just a number," or "you are as old as you feel." Conversation with midlife adults typically features topics related to marriage, children, professional lives, and personal health; In particular these conversations also include options for their parents as they gradually lose mobility and cognitive functions (Soliz & Fowler, 2014). Through media, midlife is portrayed as intergenerational systems with middle-aged heads of households juggling with extended and multiple generations of family (e.g., "Cosby Show," "Home Improvement," "Modern Family"), challenging intergenerational experiences at work (e.g., "The Office," "Madmen"), and the onset of health complications (e.g., experiences of patients via "ER" or "Grey's Anatomy.") As Prusak (2014) notes, such popular programming typically reinforces "ordinary people," (yet often white middle class families), as ideal sites for the challenges of child-rearing and marriage.

Resilience scholarship is inherently imbedded in the context of life events and best investigated as a process that unfolds over time (Masten & Wright, 2010. It charts the unmistakable phenomenon that people find ways to cultivate resources and develop approaches to life that allow them to thrive (or at least respond competently) to the life's stressors. Resilience frameworks acknowledge that there are not universal ways to respond to challenging life circumstances (Greve & Staudinger, 2006), and that our responses are invariably reactions to the challenges we face; that said, there are practices and patterns of lifelong development that contribute to resilience and recovery trajectories (Bonanno, 2008), that allow families, married and relationally close couples, and individuals to respond competently to challenges and in ways to promote growth.

While any time period would be viable for an investigation of how people foster resilience in the face of life events, a focus on midlife extends the conversation from historically more-emphasized time periods. Such investigations are consistent with contemporary lifespan scholarship, representing an interdisciplinary approach to studying people possessing multidimensionality, plasticity, and transformational aspects (Baltes, 1997; Erikson, 1950; Rutter, 2007). Furthermore, research suggests that this time period is inundated with a variety of life events that could qualify as psychological trauma (Smith & Hayslip, 2012), and therefore warranting targeted scholarly attention. Thus, the purpose of this chapter is provide a perspective on the midlife period as viewed through contemporary resilience theory, as well as propose a model for communication and interdisciplinary scholars interested in communication phenomena to organize subsequent investigations.

Middle-Age Experiences

As expressed throughout this monograph, midlife is a unique time period for those objectively aged between 40 and 60, or 65. Regardless, this time period in life is typically marked by unique experiences with work responsibilities and complex personal, relational (often marriages), and family relationships across multiple generations. Typically these years mark opportunities for greater levels of responsibility in one's career, career-switches, or returns to education for additional opportunities (Chapter 3). At home, these individuals are well imbedded in social systems where they possess a dual responsibly, known as the "sandwich generation": Caregiver to both children and potentially aging parents (Soliz & Fowler, 2014). Additional challenges typically include the infamous (yet infrequent) "midlife crisis," financial pressures, sexual health, delayed retirement, as well as issues with children, including the "empty nest"

(Henry & Miller, 2004; Waldron & Kelley, 2009). These acute challenges neglect the complications that also arise from daily stressors: interpersonal tensions, work/education, home finances, health/accident related, network issues (Almeida & Horn, 2002). While such stressors are experienced at other periods in life, they may be magnified for midlife adults because they are often decision-makers for others, as well as themselves. For example, they may be asked to manage the health of an aging parent.

These varied demands present opportunities for resilience and thriving. In fact this is also a period marked by profound meaning. Children are typically in high school and may be preparing for college and career, marking an important stage in their development toward adulthood. This maturation process fosters more independence, which can be both freeing and anxiety-provoking for parents. Careers are beginning to hit moments of greater levels of salary and responsibility, affording financial opportunities and task-choice perhaps not felt in early stages of life. Consistent with socioemotional selectivity theory (Carstensen, 1992), family and close friends provide increasingly more satisfaction and worthwhile exchanges, promoting more meaningful social experiences. In concert with lifespan theorizing, these successes mark continuance and evolving senses of wellbeing and meaning in life through protecting, coping, and growing (see Chapters 4–6).

Theorists have characterized this period as part of a larger lifespan continuum of change and transformation. Erikson's model of psychosocial development (1950) centered on the concept of *epigenesis*, that there is a sequential development of one's biological and psychological processes. As the challenges presented in one phase of life are successfully passed, individuals move on to the experiences and challenges of the next lifespan phase. In this way, middle adulthood is portrayed as a period marked with the conflict of generativity versus stagnation. Generativity is the sense of wellbeing derived from purposefulness, productivity, support, and encouragement of the next generation (Erikson, 1950). The alternative, stagnation, represents a disconnection, lack of social enrichment, and being overly absorbed in personal needs.

It is important to acknowledge that according to Erikson (1950), middle adulthood is imbedded between early adulthood and later adulthood. This recognizes the continuity and eventuality that choices in previous life stages have on subsequent ones. For example, marriage, parenting and professional choices during early adulthood have implications for the same in middle adulthood (and thus achievement of generativity). As such, those in midlife are typically married, providing for multiple generations of family members, while navigating the challenges in their working life (that enable provisioning). As Erikson has suggested, this is the enduring challenge at this time: Feeling as if one can provide a life (and hopefully a better life) for one's charges in the face of acute, daily, chronic, and developmental stressors. Given the awareness and information to navigate these challenges accordingly, how should people best maintain levels of successful aging? What separates those that age optimally from those that respond poorly to the multitude of midlife stressors?

Resilience Theory, Broadly Cast

Aptly described by Reich, Zautra, and Hall (2010) as a "paradigm shift" in the understanding of human development and social phenomena, research into resilience and related concepts represents an alternative direction for investigations in the social sciences. Resilience is typically regarded as the general processes associated with successful stressor management, or the combination of personal and social characteristics that allow a relationship or social group to deal with serious stressors in manageable way (Beck, 2016; Lucas & Buzzanell, 2012; Masten & Powell, 2003). Across the lifespan, this is a process of anticipation, adaptation, flexibility, and involving the "plasticity of human development" (Greve & Staudinger, 2006, p. 810). Given the changing state of one in relation to their social world, what developmentally works in one time period may have diminished efficacy in another. Further, plasticity suggests the ability to respond to various challenges across contexts while preserving desired aspects of the individual relationship (e.g., health, relationship quality) (Baltes, 1987; Greve & Staudinger, 2006). This infers the inherent potential of falling short or alternatively maximizing *capacity* to respond to life stressors (Bonanno, 2008; MacPhee, Lunkenheimer, & Riggs, 2015; Patterson, 2002).

An emphasis on building capacity and positive development represents an alternative to prevailing "disease" or deficit" models of psychology and related disciplines (see Shatte, Seligman, Gillham, & Reivich, 2005). As one of the original three missions of psychologists, positive emphases on human function have only recently gathered momentum (Peterson, 2006; Seligman & Csikszentmihalyi, 2000). Such work emphasizes human potential, character, strengths, developing positive mindsets, and relishing human experiences. Within the communication field research of this kind has mushroomed, as evidenced by edited volumes, book series, and conferences on such topics as positivity, character, happiness, hope, grit, and resilience (see Socha & Pitts, 2012).

Research into resilience has a slightly longer tradition within the child psychology and human development scholarship. Initial investigations examined the factors that distinguish children that emerge from challenging living circumstances (e.g., poverty, domestic abuse, absence of either or both parents) with limited or no negative results than from those with much more compromised experiences (Garmezy, 1991; Garmezy & Rutter, 1983; Luthar, 2006). Eventually this work expanded to additional contexts, circumstances, individuals, and the assessment of the object of study being resilient (e.g., what indicates a resilient community). At this stage of theory development, there had been a plurality of investigations into the concept (for reviews, see Carr, 2015; Masten & Wright, 2010; Richardson, 2002). Current theorizing emphasizes the importance of viewing resilience as a process imbedded in context (Greve & Staudinger, 2006), especially investigations within the communication field (Beck, 2016; Buzzanell, 2010; Lucas & Buzzanell, 2012). This extends to focused investigations of resilience within specific relationship types, like family (Lucas & Buzzanell, 2012; Patterson, 2002; Wilson, Chernichky, Wilkum, & Owlett, 2014) and relational resilience (Beck, 2016; this volume).

Resilience Components

Resilience is typically evidenced by the presence of three contributors: At least one challenging circumstance (i.e., stressor, risk factor), a desirable outcome worth preserving, and factors that help protect or promote a positive response (Luthar, 2006; Masten & Coatsworth, 1998; Masten & Wright, 2010). Given that negative experiences are associated with discomfort or reduced senses of wellbeing and happiness, the majority of resilience research focuses on promotive and protective resilience factors. *Promotive factors* tend to represent positive features of the individual and social context that contribute to diminishing the impact of the stressor, accentuate competencies that counteract the stressor, or strengths that overshadow or compensate for the presence of the stressor. *Protective factors*, as a more specific form of promotive factors, buffer the impact of the stressor on outcomes, and are typically measured by moderation analysis (denoting questions of what happens "when" the stressor is present or not) (Zimmerman & Brenner, 2010). For example, some social connections or community resources may be marginally beneficial to relational partners and families when stressor levels are lower (e.g., women's shelters, emergency resources), but when the stressor is high activate to promote wellbeing or minimize the impact of the stressor (providing care, medical treatment).

Importantly these contributors are imbedded in a larger sense of social, historical, and lifespan context that informed the identification of resilience (e.g., Bronfenbrenner, 1979, 1986; Greve & Staudinger, 2006), akin to developmental approaches (Baltes, 1997; Lerner, Jacobs, & Wertlieb, 2005). Masten and Wright (2010) suggest:

> There are many interacting systems that play a role in human development and resilience during or following threatening experiences and, as a consequence, many systems and levels in which assts and protective processes can be considered and targeted to boost the odds for resilience. These systems include family, school and work, religious and other cultural contexts, community organizations, and both governmental and nongovernmental organizations. (p. 230)

We may generally want to recover or bounce back from challenging life events, but what constitutes recovery for this particular context? In this context, what resources are both available and relevant? How does the stressor represent something novel or chronically experienced within the history of the community or group being investigated?

Resilience Components, *Plus Time*

What follows is an early effort to articulate a communication-centric perspective, drawing upon resilience viewed as process. Inspiration for this model was derived from Bonanno (2004), Masten and Wright (2010), Zimmerman and Brenner (2010), and preexisting models proposed by Smith and Hayslip (2012) and Aldwin and Igarashi (2012). The following *integrated communication resilience model* (ICRM) attempts to capture particular contributions and opportunities regarding communication that help clarify how resilience functions across the lifespan (and with midlife in particular).

The ICRM model is grounded in communication models emphasizing transactional processes (Barnlund, 2008), highlighting various components that are at play in fostering communication patterns across different channels (e.g., face-to-face, online). Further, the model acknowledges that this process is a part of larger interdependent social systems (Bowen, 1974). Thus aspects of the ICRM model provide the potential for an extended process of reflections and subsequent, improved resilience processes across interactions and exposure. In other words, our perceptions of the stressor and the resources we have to deal with it may be informed by our experiences and the changing nature of the world we live in. In this way, not only do various relationship-promoting message strategies serve as potential contributors toward successful stressor management, entire experiences can serve as models for future actions toward similar situations. This reflective aspect, when viewed within a lifespan and resilience perspective that suggests that both are inherently relational (Luthar, 2006), accounts for a unique communication-based role in resilience. What follows is a parsing of various features of the model, with particular attention to aspects related to communication and experiences at midlife.

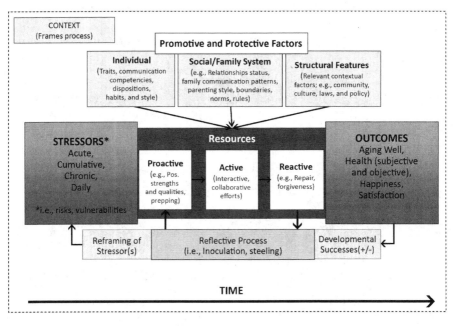

Model: Integrated Communication Resilience Model (ICRM).

Stressors

According to resilience theory, investigations into the nature of resilience necessitate the acknowledgement of some stressor that we develop resilience in relation to. Stressors, also regarded as risk factors within the child development literature, are significant disruptions to optimal processing (Grieve &

Staudinger, 2006; Masten & Wright, 2010). As described in this volume, and articulated in the Social Readjustment Rating Scale (SRRS; Holmes & Rahe, 1967), typical acute concerns for adults include death of spouse, death of family members, imprisonment, marital separation, dismissal from work, relocation, sexual difficulties, and many more (also see Chapter 3, this volume). This scale also features a "non-adult" version, that serves to further distinguish between the developmental differences and distributed family responsibilities for those in middle life and earlier stages in life (non-adult life events: e.g., death of parent, acquiring a visual deformity, change in acceptance by peers, failure of a grade in school, beginning to date). Failure to address these stressors could result in enduring vulnerabilities (Karney & Bradbury, 1995) that contribute to the onset of other relational challenges, compromise responses with resources, and overall contribute to the decline of desired relational qualities.

Contemporary communication scholarship focuses on such midlife challenges as divorce (Afifi & Keith, 2004; Frisby, Booth-Butterfield, Dillow, Martin, & Weber, 2012), employment changes (Beck, 2016; Lucas & Buzzanell, 2012), and a host of other family and relational stressors (see Beck & Socha, 2015). Across this research, it is acknowledged that stressors often transform and may therefore invoke corresponding changes in protective responses from the individual and social system. Additionally, there is a need to account for the development of maturity with a particular circumstance, and how gaining experience may in itself help to manage the stressor. For example, watching one child transition from home to college provides lessons and emotional readiness for the transition of subsequent children. Thus, this reflective process acknowledges how repeated exposure and garnering experience can transform the perception of stressors, permitting individuals and social systems to responding differently than before, with maturity and experience.

Outcomes

Stressors often are noted as such due to their tendency to impact some goal, desired state, or outcome. The most general measurements for determining an optimally lived life have been happiness, absence of negative outcomes, and satisfaction with life (either generally, or within specific contexts such as relational, family, or workplace) (Smith & Hayslip, 2012; Walsh, 2012). The measurements, due to contextual considerations across the lifespan, do not always apply universally (Kaplan, 2006). For example, satisfaction within work or relationships will likely be very different to those in their 20s versus 50s.

Expectations for merit and seniority are different, as well as what one values in a determination of "successful" or "optimal."

Thus, common in the lifespan literature is the idea of "aging well," or pursuing personal wellness as viable outcomes for those invoking a lifespan framework (Vaillant, 2002). According to Rowe and Kahn (1998) this is a combination of a) minimizing disease and disability, b) maximizing physical and cognitive abilities, and c) engaging in an active life. For midlife, this can either be framed in relation to developmental crises or tasks that are being addressed, or the response to acute stressors as they occur. While transformation and dramatic changes in one's social and professional domains are more common in earlier phases of life, research suggests that greater stability and less emotional reactivity are hallmarks of middle and later adult life (Greve & Staudinger, 2006). Invariably, goals for living well necessarily adjust as one progresses into older age, based on available resources, and are explained through utilization of selection, optimization, and compensation (SOC) life-management strategies (Jopp & Smith, 2006). Decreasing of physical mobility for example, may lead to alternative ways to interact with children and grandchildren like mediated technologies (e.g., Skype, gaming). Thus adjusting one's goals relative to what is possible allows for one to still foster relational resilience, while promoting flexibility and adaptation to changing circumstances.

Therefore, resilience is evidenced in part when a stressor minimally impacts some quality of life. Investigations of resilience traditionally identify homogeneous groups that were only distinguishable by how they performed on some outcome measure (e.g., school performance) despite risk factors (e.g., poverty) (e.g., Garmezy, 1991). Bonanno (2008) clarified that the identification of a resilience pattern (i.e., mild disruptions following the stressor) is distinct from other responses: post-traumatic growth (e.g., outcome measurements are higher after the stressor), recovery (i.e., observable elevations in symptoms that gradually return to baseline levels), delayed (i.e., lower levels of psychopathology that grew worse over time), and chronic dysfunction (i.e., development of reoccurring pathological issues). Such drastic differences to the same stressor have been generally investigated as the result of the presence and utilization of various coping resources.

Resources

The resources available to those in midlife can be evaluated as a set of internal assets and external resources situated within the larger socio-ecological system (Masten & Wright, 2010; Zimmerman & Brenner, 2010). Resilience is not just a product of individual traits, but is linked to a broader set of social and contextual variables. In particular, an ecological approach helps clarify the "widespread consensus that three major categories of protective factors exist for both children and adults: 1) individual attributes, 2) quality interpersonal relationships, and 3) environmental (or structural) supports" (Smith & Hayslip, 2012, p. 9). These layers of resources contribute to the potential to produce resilience in the light of serious stressors.

How do these resources factor into the resilience process? From a communication perspective, it helps if we consider the experience of the stressor and the response as a sequence of events that inherently involves the perception of the stressor as credible and the desired outcome as in jeopardy. At that point there is an inherently relational process involving the coordination of various resources to apply to the experience of the stressor: proactive/preventative, active, reactive/repair. Depending on the context and nature of the stressor, these phases of response may not be entirely mutually exclusive, and may in fact be perceived to happen simultaneously. Consider chronic stressors (e.g., ongoing struggles with a disease) or acute stressors (e.g., automobile accident), where one or more of the resources phases may be brief (e.g., actively trying to avoid collision), or extended (e.g., grieving and adjustment after separation). Regardless, it's useful to think about these distinct phases as they help establish frames for communication research and intervention.

Proactive resources draw upon prior experiences, deliberative preventative actions, or relevant stories and lessons to prepare for the occurrence of a stressor. Invoking the framework of positive psychology, we are fostering desirable states, strengths or conditions that help set a stable foundation for future positive or negative experiences. This could fit within "positive sentiment override," such that positive expectations in a relationship create a context for viewing future relationship events (Floyd & Markman, 1983; Story et al., 2007). This volume addresses some of these positive expectations or beliefs by suggesting that couples fostered resilience through resilient identities, and described themselves as determined, prepared, loving, patient, and truthful (Chapter 4). A couple that invokes such language to shape their shared identities also invokes expectations and scripts that correspond with couples that could be described as having grit, or bullheadedness. Beck (2016) found similar promotive qualities in his study of resilience in the face of involuntary job loss: Participants responded that their sense of partnership or togetherness, civility, and willingness to find lighter moments to enjoy each other's company contributed to how much commitment and satisfaction they felt.

More practical proactive resources including "rainy day savings" (e.g., most economists and financial consultants recommend a minimum reserve of three months salary), regular health checkups, recommended nutrition and regular exercise, meditation and mindfulness, and maintaining a positive disposition in life (e.g., optimism, hopeful mindsets). Within an ecological framework, these assets and resources can be actively cultivated, maintained, and nurtured as a byproduct of just "good living." Aside from deliberative goals and plans to improve one's life, these day-to-day actions suggest a kind of metaphorical "autopilot" that manifests in routine and daily habits.

Active resources bring to mind a "fighter pilot" metaphor, or disengagment of auto-pilot to take more of an mindful and deliberative approach not only with tasks directly related to engaging the stressor (e.g., speaking with primary caregivers, negotiating with debt collectors), but also others within one's social network and community. This category can be seen as similar to *adaptive processes* (Karney & Bradbury, 1995) suggesting the willingness and ability to engage in problem solving conversations (see Chapters 1 and 4). For example, in the event of extreme weather, community members develop emergency plans proactively, and then enact these plans with each other throughout the course of the event. Throughout the course of conflict episodes, parties will (ideally) engage in interaction that seeks to convey empathy and understanding, while striving for solutions that best represent the values of all parties (thus, a "win-win"; see Wilmot & Hocker, 2013).

Reactive resources are often regarded as repairing or restoring the individual, relationship, or larger social system to some desired level of post-stressor functioning that may or may not be feasible. Violations of trust may transform many of the assumptions that a relationship was proactively built upon (i.e., the proverbial "shaking one's beliefs to the foundation"), challenging forgiveness and reconciliation; conversely it may offer the opportunity for relationship negotiation and transition (Waldron & Kelley, 2008). For example, conversations about job loss may lead to the rediscovery of family and a sense of partnership abandoned in the pursuit of personal professional goals (Beck, 2016; Lucas & Buzzanell, 2010). Related, communities experiencing tragedy and loss related to extreme weather events (e.g., hurricanes, tornados, tsunamis) may emerge with a better sense or collective awareness of needs in the community as well as weaknesses that exist in the infrastructure and disaster management plans (Gunderson, 2000; Merolla, 2015). In the truest sense of a process-based and iterative nature associated with resilience, these reactive moments create opportunities to then prepare with great levels of efficacy for future events. In other words, the reactive can initiate a cyclical and eventually proactive resilience process.

Additional Implications of *Time*

Part of the iterative nature of resilience is embracing that there is a momentary process of assessment and application going on in relation to the experience of challenging circumstances. As mentioned above, thinking of the resilience process as episodic (i.e. proactive, active, and reactive) helps us clarify how the use of communication resources can set the scene, navigate the experience, and inform its resolution or transformation. Importantly, while such distinct episodic labels may suit very defined stressor episodes (e.g., extreme weather events), more typically these phases are overlapping and mutually influential (e.g., the reaction leads to proactive efforts to not experience the same stressor the same way). In this way, we cultivate wisdom, experience, and familiarity with the circumstances of our changing lives. Indeed, intermittent exposure to stress or challenges enhances arousal regulation and resilience: A phenomenon also referred to as steeling or toughening (Rutter, 2007). Additionally, weathering challenges across time together is regarded as an experience-gaining process inherent to the human condition (Kaplan, 2006), and a characteristic present in strong families (Walsh, 2012).

In the incremental, directional sense, acknowledging time promotes the idea that memory and coordinated goals provide context for how resilience fits into the larger context of one's lifespan. Moments stretch out to larger time periods, episodes punctuate larger patterns of experiences we use to characterize places and people, and chapters or turning points serve as useful metaphors for expressing changes that occur in what we believed we would become and what we have. Resilience however, is not merely a momentary interaction, but instead a larger and extended process (in each direction from that moment) (Smith & Hayslip, 2012). Further, the accumulation of stressors or risks (which often don't wait their turn) may be too much for one person or system to adequately handle (e.g., total devastation following extreme weather events; compounding issues related to health complications and loss of a family member).

Future Research and Applications

For those interested in research utilizing resilience theory, there is a wealth of interdisciplinary and communication-based research available. Child development scholars, psychologists, and sociologists have done much of the initial work and subsequent organizational meta-theoretical conversations (see Masten & Wright, 2010; Richardson, 2002). Communication scholarship on resilience draws from coping, relational maintenance and social support research (Afifi, Merrill, & Davis, 2015; Beck, 2016) and tends to be imbedded within families and communities (Buzzanell, 2000; Carr, 2015; Lucas & Buzzanell, 2012; Wilson & Gettings, 2012; Wilson et al., 2014). Steps have been made to "circle the wagons" of related scholarship, represented by an edited volume relating to experiences of both hope and resilience (Beck & Socha, 2015). There are undoubtedly other studies unmentioned, as well as ones still emerging that will further illuminate the potential directions for both communication scholarship as well as those interested in communication phenomena. What follows is an attempt to channel this chapter into some viable next directions for both research and practice.

For Research

The increased adoption of this theory to help explain more complex, transformative, and multifaceted phenomena should be of interest to scholars of interpersonal, organization, health, and family communication. For a lifespan communication-based resilience model to take hold: "communication needs to take a more central place in the theoretical structure ... mak(ing) communication the phenomenon central to our discussion" (Harwood, 2014, p. 23). The ICRM model presented in this chapter attempted to provide an avenue for this to happen on multiple ecological and processual levels. Indeed, our investigations of communication phenomena can manifest in the model as a communication based-stressor (e.g., cyberbullying, toxic work environment), a combination of personal dispositions (e.g., optimism, mindfulness) and social resources (e.g., perceived and received social support, forms of positive communication), as well as desired outcomes that reflect preferred characterizations of our families, relationships, and social groups' communication practices (e.g., relationship quality, satisfaction)

Communication scholars should take particular interest in what aspects of interaction in our various settings and relationships contributes to resilience.

This likely comes down to a careful inventory of what promotive and protective factors are relevant to the relationship and context under investigation. Is it as simple as expressing a greater ratio of positivity to negativity (Fredrickson & Losada, 2005), or any message characterized as positive, uplifting, or supportive? What about how such resources are utilized in proactive, active, and reactive ways? Are there circumstances where such communication fails, is ineffectively delivered, or the nature of the relationship doesn't suggest such communication is appropriate or sincere? How would that affect the process of resilience, at various stages of the process, and in subsequent revisitations of the stressor? Gerontologists Smith and Hayslip (2012) contend, "… it may be fruitful to explore resilience as … an attribute defined by the quality of individuals' interactions with each other" (p. 17). This suggests that resilience is a product of specific interdependent features of interpersonal and family communication, as contributed by the contributing members of the system. Consider how health diagnoses shape the lives not just of the diagnosed, but of caregivers, family and friends, as well as sources of assistance from the community (e.g., treatment centers, social workers, emergency personnel). Dyadic investigations and separated couple interview studies (or patient-secondary care-giver) would be particularly relevant here.

Context is a largely inseparable aspect of resilience research that helps define what resilience is being generated (and measured) in relation to, but also for generalizing or accurately attributing our findings to relevant populations. Acknowledging that our investigations are essentially "development in context" (Greve & Staudinger, 2006, p. 798) provides greater accuracy as to what works and when, for what reasons. Context also allows us to understand and acknowledging common resources associated with this population, towards these relevant and developmentally appropriate goals. Such an approach affords the opportunity to savor the rich investigations, regardless of quantitative or qualitative methodological choice, embedded in context that such a theory affords. To researchers, this suggests a careful acknowledgement of aspects of the social, physical, and historical circumstances that surround the populations we want to investigate: For example, we aren't just investigating individuals experiencing job loss alone, but being mindful of the extended challenges and even resources possible from those closest and most invested (Beck, 2016; Lucas & Buzzanell, 2012).

Lastly, midlife resilience is part and parcel of time. Besides the interview approach reported in this monograph, there are number of ways that scholars have investigated phenomena that change with time, including but not limited to longitudinal surveys (e.g., Vaillant, 2002), life story narratives (Clausen, 1998), retrospective interview techniques (Baxter & Bullis, 1986; Huston et al., 1981), cross-sectional comparison studies (Sugarman, 2001), diary studies (e.g., Iowa Communication Record: Duck, Rutt, Hoy, & Strejc, 1991). Tracking turning points remains a viable means for investigating lifespan phenomena, and especially at midlife (Assink & Schroots, 2009; Baxter & Bullis, 1986; Pitts & Hummert, 2012; Wethington, Kessler, & Pixley, 2004). Finally, midlife resilience research would benefit from additional investigations into daily stressors and responses (e.g., Almeida & Horn, 2002), which are also sites for daily, incremental experiences of resilience in adulthood (Ong, Bergeman, Bisconti, & Wallace, 2006). Diary methods or experiential sampling methodologies provide viable means to learn more about situated communication and daily communication and affective patterns (e.g., human flourishing: Fredrickson & Losada, 2005).

For Practice

Masten and Wright (2010) contend that "… there are several basic strategies for intervention: a) reducing risk (e.g., prenatal care to prevent premature birth, removing landmines to prevent injuries to a population), b) increasing assets or resources (e.g., provision of food programs, employment counselors), and c) mobilizing powerful protective systems (e.g., improving the effectiveness of parents, nurturing the leadership of young people in rebuilding a community after disaster or war" (p. 230). These three possibilities need not be exclusive, but possibly a part of a broader intervention and engagement. Thus when considering strategies for developing midlife resilience, we are ultimately making a decision about the potential impact and feasibility of the intervention in relation to the goals we hope to achieve.

While there are many examples of lifespan and resilience interventions in the literature (see Sugarman, 2001), the Penn Resiliency Program (Shatte et al., 2005) stands out as an interventional program with a number of skill modules that reflect cognitive and social competences that have lifespan potential. Despite being originally designed for children with depression, the program saw improvement in those with and without such symptoms. Thus such a program is in many ways proactively helping to build a stronger foundation for subsequent challenges in life, while also providing active strategies of conflict management, negotiation techniques, and social problem solving. Given that so many of the examples from this program have to do with children's relationships with family members and in educational settings, working with adults or designing an adult version to complement the children's curriculum would be a way to extend this program across the lifespan.

Applications at midlife would promote our ability to perceive challenges in manageable ways, provide the necessary tools for cultivating personal mindset and supportive social networks, while also learning and reflecting on whatever the result may be. Adapting an open-minded approach that challenges are inevitable and that we can lean on others in times of need sounds simple (Beck & Socha, 2015), but not if we retreat internally and stagnate (a tendency of some at midlife). Programs like the Penn Resilience Program, or perhaps just informally taking a moment (or a weekend) in your own relationship to cherish each other and celebrate two lives in concert and cooperation, helps keep life focused on those optimal states of existence we should all be striving for.

Conclusion

As a "last uncharted territory" (Brim et al., 2004) midlife adulthood represents a unique opportunity for scholars interested in positive communication and related phenomena. Considered along with the increasing interest in resilience as indicative of a "paradigm shift" for investigations into human well being and potential (Reich et al., 2012) this long neglected period of the lifespan may benefit from additional interest in what helps contribute to thriving at midlife. Communication researchers are especially well positioned to call attention to both the various contributors to and reflective nature of the resilience process imbedded within context.

References

Afifi, T. D., & Keith, S. (2004). A risk and resiliency model of ambiguous loss in post-divorce stepfamilies. *Journal of Family Communication, 4*, 65–98. Retrieved from http://dx.doi.org/10.1207/s15327698jfc0402_1

Afifi, T. D., Merrill, A. F., & Davis, S. (2015, May). *The theory of resilience and relational load.* Paper presented at the annual meeting of the International Communication Association, San Juan, Puerto Rico.

Aldwin, C. M., & Igarashi, H. (2012). An ecological model of resilience in late life. *Annual Review of Gerontology/Geriatric, 32*, 115–130. Retrieved from http://dx.doi.org/1891/0198-8794.32.115

Almeida, D. M., & Horn, M. C. (2002). Is daily life more stressful during middle adult-hood? In O. G. Brim, C. D. Ryff, & R. C. Kessler (Eds.), *How healthy are we? A national study of well-being at midlife* (pp. 425–451). Chicago, IL: The University of Chicago Press.

Assink, H. J., & Schroots, J. J. (2009). *The dynamics of autobiographical memory: Using the LIM.* Cambridge: Hogrefe Publishing.

Baltes, P. B. (1987). Theoretical propositions of life-span developmental psychology: On the dynamics between growth and decline. Developmental Psychology, 23, 611–696.

Baltes, P. B. (1997). On the incomplete architecture of human ontogeny: Selection, optimiza-tion and compensation as foundation of developmental theory. *American Psychologist, 52*, 366–380.

Barnlund, D. C. (2008). A transactional model of communication. In C. D. Mortensen (Ed.), *Communication theory* (2nd ed., pp. 47–57). New Brunswick, NJ: Transaction.

Baxter, L. A., & Bullis, C. (1986). Turning points in developing romantic relationships. *Human Communication Research, 12*(4), 469–493.

Beck, G. A. (2016). Surviving involuntary unemployment together: The role of resilience-pro-moting communication in familial and committed relationships. *Journal of Family Com-munication, 16*(4), 369–385.

Beck, G. A., & Socha, T. J. (Eds.). (2015). *Communication hope and resilience across the lifespan.* New York, NY: Peter Lang.

Bonanno, G. A. (2008). Loss, trauma, and human resilience: Have we underestimated the human capacity to thrive after extremely aversive events. *Psychological Trauma, S*(1), 101–113.

Bowen, M. (1974). Alcoholism as viewed through family systems theory and family psy-chotherapy. *Annals of the New York Academy of Sciences, 233*, 115–122. doi:10.1111/j.1749-6632.1974.tb40288.x

Brim, O. G., Ryff, C. D., & Kessler, R. C. (2004). *How healthy are we? A national study of well-be-ing at midlife.* Chicago, IL: The University of Chicago Press.

Bronfenbrenner, U. (1979). *The ecology of human development: Experiments by nature and design.* Cambridge, MA: Harvard University Press.

Bronfenbrenner, U. (1986). Ecology of the family as a context for human development: Research perspectives. *Developmental Psychopathology, 22*(6), 723–742.

Buzzanell, P. M. (2010). Presidential address—Resilience: Talking, resisting, and imagining, new normalcies into being. *Journal of Communication, 60*, 1–14.

Carr, K. (2015). Communication and family resilience. In C. R. Berger & M. E. Roloff (Eds.), *International encyclopedia of interpersonal communication* (pp. 1–9). Hoboken, NJ: Wiley Blackwell. Retrieved from http://dx.doi.org/10.1002/9781118540190

Carstensen. L. L. (1992). Social and emotional patterns in adulthood: Support for socio-emo-tional selectivity theory. *Psychology & Aging, 7*, 331–338.

Clausen, J. A. (1998). Life reviews and life stories. In J. Z. Giele & G. H. Elder Jr. (Eds.), *Meth-ods of life course research: Qualitative and quantitative approaches* (pp. 189–212). Thousand Oaks, CA: Sage.

Duck, S., Rutt, D. J., Hoy, M., & Strejc H. H. (1991). Some evident truths about conversations in everyday relationships: All communications are not created equal. *Human Communication Research, 18*(2), 228–267. Retrieved from http://dx.doi.org/10.1111/j.1468-2958.1991.tb00545.x

Erikson, E. H. (1950). *Childhood and society*. New York, NY: Norton.

Floyd, F. J., & Markman, H. J. (1983). Observational biases in spouse observation: Toward a cognitive/behavioral model of marriage. *Journal of Consulting and Clinical Psychology, 51*, 450–457.

Fredrickson, B. L., & Losada, M. F. (2005). Positive affect and the complex dynamics of human flourishing. *American Psychologist, 60*(7), 678–686. Retrieved from http://dx.doi.org/10.1037/0003-066X.60.7.678

Frisby, B. N., Booth-Butterfield, M., Dillow, M. R., Martin, M., & Weber, K. (2012). Face and resilience in divorce: The impact on emotions, stress, and post-divorce relationships. *Journal of Social and Personal Relationships, 29*(6), 715–735. Retrieved from http://dx.doi.org/10.1177/0265407512443452

Garmezy, N. (1991). Resiliency and vulnerability to adverse developmental outcomes associated with poverty. *American Behavioral Scientist, 34*, 416–430.

Garmezy, N., & Rutter, M. (1983). *Stress, coping, and development in children*. New York, NY: McGraw-Hill.

Greve, W., & Staudinger, U. M. (2006). Resilience in later adulthood and old age: Resources and potentials for successful aging. In D. Cicchetti & A. Cohen (Eds.), *Developmental Psychopathology* (2nd ed., pp. 796–840). New York, NY: Wiley.

Gunderson, L. H. (2000). Ecological resilience in theory and application. *Annual Review of Ecological Systems, 31*, 425–439.

Harwood, J. (2014). Lifespan communication theory. In J. F. Nussbaum (Ed.), *The handbook of lifespan communication* (pp. 9–27). New York, NY: Peter Lang.

Henry, R. G., & Miller, R. B. (2004). Marital problems occurring in midlife: Implications for couples therapists. *American Journal of Family Therapy, 32*(5), 405–417.

Holmes, T. H., & Rahe R. H. (1967). The social readjustment rating scale. *Journal of Psychosomatic Research, 11*(2), 213–218. Retrieved from http://dx.doi.org/10.1016/0022-3999(67)90010-4

Huston, T. L., Surra, C., Fitzgerald, N., & Cate, R. (1981). From courtship to marriage: Mate selection as an interpersonal process. In S. Duck & R. Gilmour (Eds.), *The emerging field of personal relationships* (pp. 53–88). New York, NY: Academic Press.

Jopp, D., & Smith, J. (2006). Resources and life-management strategies as determinants of successful aging: On the protective effect of selection, optimization, and compensation. *Psychology & Aging, 21*(2), 253–265.

Kaplan, H. B. (2006). Understanding the concept of resilience. In S. Goldstein & R. B. Brooks (Eds.), *Handbook of resilience in children* (pp. 39–47). New York, NY: Springer.

Karney, B. R., & Bradbury, T. N. (1995). The longitudinal course of marital quality and stability: A review of theory, method, and research. *Psychological Bulletin, 118*(1), 3–34.

Lerner, R. M., Jacobs, F., & Wertlieb, D. (2005). *Applied developmental science: An advanced textbook*. Thousand Oaks, CA: Sage Publications.

Longstaff, P. H. (2005). *Security, resilience, and communication in unpredictable environments such as terrorism, natural disaster, and complex technology.* Cambridge, MA: Harvard University Program on Information Resources Policy.

Lucas, K., & Buzzanell, P. M. (2012). Memorable messages of hard times: Constructing short and long-term resiliencies through family communication. *Journal of Family Communication, 12,* 189–208.

Luthar, S. S. (2006). Resilience in development: A synthesis of research across five decades. In D. Cicchetti & D. J. Cohen (Eds.), *Developmental psychopathology. Volume 3. Risk, disorder, and adaptation* (2nd ed., pp. 739–795). New York, NY: Wiley.

MacPhee, D., Lunkenheimer, E., & Riggs, N. (2015). Resilience as regulation of family and developmental processes. *Family Relations, 64,* 153–175.

Mancini, A. D., & Bonnano, G. A. (2010). Resilience to potential trauma: Toward a lifespan approach. In J. W. Reich, A. J. Zautra, & J. S. Hall (Eds.), *Handbook of adult resilience* (pp. 258–280). New York, NY: Guilford Press.

Masten, A. S. (2001). Ordinary magic: Resilience processes in development. *American Psychologist, 56*(3), 227–238.

Masten, A. S., & Coatsworth, J. D. (1998). The development of competence in favorable and unfavorable environments: Lessons from research on successful children. *American Psychologist, 53*(2), 205–220.

Masten, A. S., & Powell, J. L. (2003). A resilience framework for research, policy, and practice. In Suniya S. Luthar (Ed.) *Resilience and Vulnerability: Adaptation in the Context of Childhood Adversities. (pp. 1–25).* New York: Cambridge University Press.

Masten, A. S., & Wright, M. O. (2010). Resilience over the lifespan: Developmental perspectives on resistance, recovery, and transformation. In J. W. Reich, A. J. Zautra, & J. S. Hall (Eds.), *Handbook of adult resilience* (pp. 258–280). New York, NY: Guilford Press.

Merolla, A. J. (2015). When all seems lost: Building hope through communication after natural disasters. In G. A. Beck & T. J. Socha (Eds.), *Communicating hope and resilience across the lifespan* (pp. 176–194). New York, NY: Peter Lang.

Ong, A. D., Bergeman, C. S., Bisconti, T. L., & Wallace, K. A. (2006). Psychological resilience, positive emotions, and successful adaptation to stress in later life. *Journal of Personality and Social Psychology, 91*(4), 730–749.

Patterson, J. (2002). Understanding family resilience. *Journal of Clinical Psychology, 58*(3), 233–246.

Peterson, C. (2006). *A primer in positive psychology.* New York: Oxford University Press.

Pitts, M. J., & Hummert, M. L. (2014). Lifespan communication methodology. In J. F. Nussbaum (Ed.), *The handbook of lifespan communication* (pp. 29–52). New York, NY: Peter Lang.

Prusak, D. T. (2014). Spouse and parent: Television images of major roles of adulthood. In J. F. Nussbaum (Ed.), *The handbook of lifespan communication* (pp. 331–347). New York, NY: Peter Lang.

Reich, W., Zautra, A. J., & Hall, J. S. (Eds.). (2010). Handbook of adult resilience. New York, NY: Guilford.

Richardson, G. E. (2002). The metatheory of resilience and resiliency. *Journal of Clinical Psychology*, 58, 307–321. Retrieved from http://dx.doi.org/10.1002/jclp.10020

Rowe, J. W., & Kahn, R. L. (1998). *Successful aging*. New York, NY: Pantheon/Random House.

Rutter, M. (2007). Resilience, competence, and coping. *Child Abuse, & Neglect, 31*(3), 205–209.

Schlein, S. (1989). *Erik Erikson, a way of looking at things: Selected papers, 1930–1980*. New York, NY: W. W. Norton & Company.

Seligman, M. E. P., & Csikszentmihalyi, M. (2000). Positive psychology: An introduction. *American Psychologist*, 55, 5–14.

Shatte, A. J., Seligman, M. E., Gillham, J. E., & Reivich, K. (2005). The role of positive psychology in child, adolescent, and family development. In R. M. Lerner, F. Jacobs, & D. Wertlieb (Eds.), *Applied developmental science: An advanced textbook* (pp. 61–80). Thousand Oaks, CA: Sage.

Smith, G. C., & Hayslip, B. (2012). Resilience in adulthood and later life: What does it mean and where are we heading? In B. Hayslip & G. C. Smith (Eds.), Annual *Review of Gerontology and Geriatrics* (pp. 3–28). New York, NY: Springer.

Socha, T. J., & Pitts, M. (Eds.) (2012). *The positive side of interpersonal communication*. New York and Bern, Switzerland: Peter Lang.

Soliz, J., & Fowler, C. (2014). Sandwich relationships: Intergenerational communication. In J. F. Nussbaum (Ed.), *The handbook of lifespan communication* (pp. 293–310). New York, NY: Peter Lang.

Story, T. N., Berg, C. A., Smith, T. W., Beveridge, R., Henry, N. J. M., & Pearce, G. (2007). Age, martial satisfaction, and optimism as predictors of positive sentiment override in middle-aged and older married couples, *Psychology and Aging, 22*(4), 719–727.

Sugarman, L. (2001). *Life-span development: Theories, concepts and interventions*. London: Routledge.

Vaillant, G. E. (2002). *Aging well*. Boston, MA: Little Brown.

Waldron, V., & Kelley, D. (2008). *Communicating forgiveness*. Thousand Oaks, CA: Sage.

Waldron, V., & Kelley, D. (2009). *Marriage at midlife: Analytical tools and counseling strategies*. New York, NY: Springer.

Walsh, F. (2012). Successful aging and family resilience. In B. Hayslip & G. C. Smith (Eds.), *Annual review of gerontology and geriatrics* (pp. 153–172). New York, NY: Springer.

Wethington, E., Kessler, R. C., & Pixley, J. E. (2004). Turning points in adulthood. In O. G. Brim, C. D. Ryff, & R. C. Kessler (Eds.), *How healthy are we? A national study of well-being at midlife* (pp. 586–613). Chicago, IL: The University of Chicago Press.

Wilmot, W., & Hocker, J. (2013). *Interpersonal conflict* (9th ed.). New York, NY: McGraw Hill.

Wilson, S. R., Chernichky, S. M., Wilkum, K., & Owlett, J. S. (2014). Do family communication patterns buffer children with difficulties associated with parent's deployment? Examining deployed and at-home parents' perspectives. *Journal of Family Communication, 14*, 32–52. Retrieved from http://dx.doi.org/10.1080/15267431.2013.857325

Wilson, S. R., & Gettings, P. (2012). Nurturing children as assets: A positive approach to preventing child maltreatment and promoting healthy youth development. In T. J. Socha & M. J. Pitts (Eds.), *The positive side of interpersonal communication* (pp. 277–296). New York, NY: Peter Lang.

Zautra, A. J., Hall, J. S., & Murray, K. E. (2010). Resilience: A new definition of health for people and communities. In J. Reich, A. Zautra, & J. Hall (Eds.), *Handbook of adult resilience* (pp. 3–29). New York, NY: Guilford Press.

Zimmerman, M. A., & Brenner, A. B. (2010). Resilience in adolescence: Overcoming neighborhood disadvantage. In J. W. Reich, A. J. Zautra, & J. S. Hall (Eds.), *Handbook of adult resilience* (pp. 283–308). New York, NY: Guilford Press.

· 8 ·

METHODS AND MEASURES

This brief chapter provides information on data collection and analysis procedures for those who want to explore the research methods used to generate the data reported in this book. I describe data collection and analysis procedures, including the root metaphor analysis that informs Chapters 4–6. The interview schedule is presented, including the questions that were used in every interview. Many of the most interesting quotations reported in earlier chapters are drawn from the observations of the student interviewers who are described in Chapter 2. In this chapter the reader will find the instructions the students were asked to follow as they reported on their observations. Whereas Chapter 2 addressed the philosophical and conceptual questions I confronted in mounting this multi-year study, the current chapter fills in details that might be of less interest to the general reader but of keen interest to students of research methods.

Data Collection Procedures

Participating couples were located via network sampling. Undergraduates enrolled in an upper-division course on communication and aging recruited qualifying couples in their social networks, including coworkers, parents of friends, and members of their own extended family. These students, who also served as interviewers, received instruction in how to conduct and record the interviewers, a detailed interview schedule, and university-sanctioned training in the protection of human research participants. Participants received a brief explanation as to the purpose of audio-recording the conversation (to achieve accuracy when reporting and interpreting the data). They were reminded that 1) this research was voluntary, 2) they could refuse to answer any question, and 3) they could terminate participation at any time without penalty. Upon agreeing, the couple signed a consent form.

Interviewers audio-recorded the interviews and also provided verbatim written reports of responses to key interview questions. They also provided a written synthesis of the interview responses and a subjective assessment of the interview process, including the comfort of the participants and their skill as an interviewer. These student-interviewer observations are also used as data in this report. For that reason, students also completed consent forms. In cases where consent was not granted, student data were discarded.

The semi-structured interview protocol included open-ended questions prompting participants to discuss the relationship's history and significant changes (see below). Demographic and rapport-building questions were asked first. "Do you have children? If so, how many? Would you tell the story of how you first met?" To help the participants focus on midlife, they were asked: "Compared to earlier years, how would you say your marriage is similar or different?" Another question asked about challenges, changes, and opportunities for growth that had been experienced over the years. A follow-up question focused again on midlife: "Please describe the challenges, changes, and opportunities for growth during the last ten years." Before concluding the interview, the participants were asked for any advice for younger couples and to add any other final thoughts or comments to the interview.

Data Analysis Procedures

The student interviewers provided detailed written reports of the interviews, with responses to key questions reported verbatim (see assignment below). These reports along with the audio recordings constituted the data for this study. The initial review of the data involved qualitative thematic analysis of 20% of all interviews (n = 54). Once coding categories were well-defined, a key word search was used to generate rough estimates of the frequency of each category across the larger sample.

Qualitative Analysis

The initial coding process involved the sample of 54 interviews. These were conducted by students in two courses randomly selected from the larger group of nine courses that had participated in the project. A coding team first analyzed the written interview reports using a six-step qualitative thematic analysis (Braun & Clarke, 2006): 1) familiarizing coders with the data, 2) generating initial codes, 3) searching for themes, 4) reviewing themes, 5) defining and naming themes, and 6) producing the report. The six members of the team worked initially in two groups of three, with each analyzing 50% of the data. One team coded for relational changes, challenges, or stressors that occurred during the middle stages of the relationship (15–35 years) and or middle age (participants were between 40 and 65 years of age). Second, they coded for adaptive relational practices (if any) that couples associated with these changes, including but not limited to those that might be labelled as preventing, resisting, coping, surviving, adjusting, growing, or thriving. After this coding round, preliminary themes and associated examples were presented to the whole research team for discussion.

The second phase of coding refined the codes and generated more comprehensive themes and resulted in the collapsing of others. The process was facilitated by the NVivo software program, which provided researchers the opportunity to explore potential relationships among coding categories using visual depictions, annotations and coding memos. The third phase of analysis involved continued use of the constant comparative method (Glaser & Strauss, 1967; Strauss & Corbin, 1998) to evaluate the adequacy of the revised category system. Each member reviewed four or five new interview reports in an effort to locate coding units that seemed not to fit as well as additional examples of those that fit well. The fourth and final coding round involved further discussion and revision of each theme by the full research team.

This coding system was then subjected to additional refinement. First the author and several additional student assistants listened to the audiotapes to check the accuracy of the student-generated reports. Second, researchers searched a randomly selected sample of ten interviews for negative cases—instances that were not covered by the original coding effort. This review yielded several new coding categories and refinements in several others.

During this phase, additional quoted material was selected from the interviews to enrich reporting of the categories.

Quantitative Analysis

The author and a student assistant conducted a key word search of the entire corpus of interview reports. The intent was to determine the frequency of the kinds of midlife adversities/ stressors reported by the couples (results are reported in Chapter 3). The method was similar to that employed by Kelley (2015) to identify instances of justice-related discourse occurring in interviews with long-term romantic couples. Using a thesaurus, the researchers generated a list of synonyms for each category of change. For example, synonyms for "illness" were sickness/sick, health problems, and disease.

The complete archive of interview reports was then searched to identify the number of interviews that included one or more of these terms. The report and the transcript were checked to make sure the usage of the word was consistent with the category. For example, the word "sick" could refer to an illness of one partner, but it might also refer to a deranged individual or disgusting brand of behavior. Of course it is possible that some less-familiar synonyms were excluded from the search. However, the process yielded a rough estimate of the percentage of couples who reported (for example) illness to be a change or challenge during the middle years of marriage. It also located additional quotations that could be used to illustrate each category.

The keyword search technique was not as useful in the search for examples of protective, coping, and optimizing practices (the subjects of Chapters 4–6), largely because the language used to describe them was more complex, variable, and ambiguous. For that reason, quantitative estimates are not provided. However, key word searching and the associated transcript checking did yield numerous additional variations on the practices identified in the original qualitative thematic analysis. Some of these examples are reported in the text.

Supplemental Method: Root Metaphor Analysis

As data analysis progressed I made two observations that led me to supplement the methods described above. First, I sensed that the categories emerging during the analysis of these data were both comprehensive (good) and numerous (perhaps not so good). Second, in listening to the discourse couples used to describe how their relationships changed, I noticed that they often used metaphorical language. This in itself is not surprising, as recent research has suggested that more than 7% of interpersonal talk is metaphorical (Steen, Dorst, Herrmann, Kaal, & Krennmayr, 2010). The methodologies of metaphor analysis have a long history in the fields of linguistics and communication studies—longer than I can fully present here (for a seminal work, see Lakoff & Johnson, 1980/2003). Metaphors are aids to sense-making, as they compare something familiar (e.g., war) to something that is ambiguous, confusing, or vexing (e.g., relational conflict). They are also used for purposes of argument, motivation, and to invite creative thinking.

Burgers (2016) has recently reviewed the role of metaphor in modelling changes in communication, arguing that change can be incremental (metaphors are adapted) or fundamental (metaphors are replaced). Most relevant to the current investigation, the introduction of certain metaphors (e.g., "tightening the belt") has been linked to resilience during times of adversity and change. A study of parents enduring difficult financial circumstances reported that they used the belt metaphor (and others) to foster resilience in their children during times of adversity, to literally talk normality into being (Lucas & Buzzanell, 2012). Indeed, resilience was long ago described as "ordinary magic" (Masten, 2001), a metaphor that emphasizes that it is both common and mysterious. Metaphors have certainly been examined for what they imply about romantic love (Glucksberg & McGlone, 1999), which has been described with such varying metaphors as "good chemistry" or "a deep connection."

These observations convinced me to be mindful of the metaphors that couples used to describe their relationships at midlife. I made notes of these metaphors as I read and reread the discourse, selecting examples that seemed most illustrative of the coding categories and noting those that failed to fit. I don't claim to have located every metaphorical expression. But I did manage to collect a large number of expressions used by these couples to make sense of their relationships. Many metaphors were referenced by multiple couples. And it became apparent that certain foundational metaphors were providing the raw symbolic material for relational sense-making.

The next step in this process was an effort to identify these underlying or "root" metaphors. A root metaphor is a basic conceptual framework upon which meanings are layered. The notion of the root, which is itself metaphorical, suggests that meaning is nurtured by, and grounded in this base. As roots grow mostly underground, root metaphors exist largely below the level of awareness. Root metaphor analysts listen carefully to the language people use to make sense of their surroundings, looking for connections among symbolic expressions. The underlying metaphor is suggestive of the world view that guides these interpretations. For example, Smith and Eisenberg (1987) examined the metaphors used by employees to describe Disneyland, their place of employment. They heard employees describing their "roles," "costumes," and the "cast." All of these terms express an understanding of their work as a theatrical performance. They concluded that in the minds of employees, Disney puts on a "show." The root metaphor, these researchers concluded, was "Disneyland is a drama" (p. 371).

By identifying root metaphors, I also hope to better understand how people re/fashion their relationships from raw symbolic materials. Given the profusion of practices described in Chapters 4–6, one of my goals was to offer a more "elegant" explanation; one grounded in a few underlying sources of meaning. In addition, metaphors highlight certain relational rationales even as they exclude others. By analyzing them I sought to understand how these rationales differed for couples who seemed to protecting themselves from adversity (Chapter 4), coping (Chapter 5) or growing (Chapter 6). I think this metaphorical language makes the data more resonant for the reader and more richly reflective of the meaning these couples created around their relationships.

The first step in the analysis was simply to list as many metaphors as possible. From there I analyzed the sets of exemplars, looking for similarities and differences in meaning. As groupings emerged, I tried to identify those that expressed or qualified a deeper, foundational concept. Those deeper concepts were identified as root metaphors.

Interview Schedule

Introduction

- *Say this*: "This interview is part of a class project for CMN 417 (Aging and Communication). One of our class topics concerns long term relationships. We are learning how partners stay together over long periods of time. Because you have been in a romantic relationship for 20 years or more, we would like to learn from your experience. This interview consists of a series of questions about the history of your relationship, key turning points in the relationship, any recent changes you have experienced, and your advice to younger people in relationships. With your permission, your answers may be shared with our class and incorporated in educational materials. In addition, your interview may be analyzed for research purposes and incorporated in published research reports. Your name and identifying details will be changed if your interview is used for these purposes."

- *Read the consent form* (attached separately) and have each participant sign to indicate their permission. If they prefer that their interview not be used for research purposes, write a note on the consent form.
- *Turn on the recorder.* Orally confirm that the participants have reviewed the permission form, signed, and granted their permission for you to record the interview and use their data.

Rapport Building/Background (Establish a Friendly Conversational Tone)

Q1: How many years have you been married (or if not married, together as a couple)?
Q2: Tell me a bit about you and your family situation.
     Do you have children? If so, how many?
     What kind of work do you do?
     How would other people describe you two?
Q3: Would you tell the story of how you first met?
Q4: What did you think about marriage (if they are married) at that time?
     Probe: Do you think people view it differently now? Do you?

Midlife Changes, Challenges and Opportunities for Growth

Interviewers: Your job in this section of the interview is to explore the *changes, challenges,* and *opportunities* for growth experienced by this couple. Follow-up to locate additional examples.
Q5: Please describe what you consider to be the most important *changes, challenges,* or *opportunities* for growth in your relationship together.
     Follow-up: *Why was this important? Do other examples come to mind?*

The Last 10 Years

Interviewers: Now focus on the most recent part of the relationship, the last ten years.

Q6: Think about how your relationship has changed during these most recent 10 years. This might include any adjustments you have made or new situations that you have encountered. Please describe changes you have noticed in your relationship in the *last 10 years*.

Probe each change: How did you adjust to these changes?

Q7: Compared to your early years together, how would you say your marriage is similar or different? Please describe.

Advice to Younger Couples

You have stayed together for a long time. Your experience may be helpful to younger couples who want to stay together for a long time.

Q8: What advice do you have for younger couples and couples who are just starting out?

Q9: Do you have anything else you would like to say about your relationship and how you have stayed together for a long time?

Demographic Data

Make sure you gather this basic information: age of each partner, ethnicity of each partner, length of marriage and relationship, number of children, current age of children, first or second marriage? *Include this data in your written report.*

Conclusion

1. *Say this:* If you have any questions or concerns about this project, please contact my instructor, Dr. Vincent Waldron at XXX-XXX-XXXX. If you feel any distress as a result of this project and would like to speak with a mental health provider, please contact Dr. Waldron.
2. *Say this:* If you would like to revoke permission to use this information, just let me know now. If you later decide to revoke permission, just call Dr. Waldron.
3. *Thank you very much for helping with this class project!*

Interview Assignment

COM 417: Long Term Relationship Interview

Student Consent

If, after reading the assignment instructions, you would prefer an alternative equivalent assignment, please contact your instructor. I encourage you to complete this assignment because it relates directly to class material and should prove useful in your own life, but you will experience no penalty if you choose the alternative assignment. Also, you can switch assignments at any time, without penalty.

With your permission, and that of your interviewees, your assignment may be analyzed for research or educational purposes. For example, any "relational turning points" you describe might be referenced in a research article or in an instructional guide for other students. You can make a note on the consent form if you choose **not** to make your report available for research purposes. Please read, sign, and submit the consent form when you submit your interview report.

Overview

You should read thoroughly the *Marriage at Midlife* text before completing this assignment.

The purpose of this assignment is to help students understand romantic relationships from a "life course" perspective. From this point of view, the current status of a relationship must be understood in terms of its historical development. The historical events and environmental factors that shaped the relationship, the partners' efforts to maintain the relationship during times of crises and normality, recent relationship adjustments, and perceptions of the relational future are important in understanding how romantic relationships evolve. A secondary purpose is to help students acquire information that may be helpful in maintaining their own romantic relationships.

Students are asked to locate two romantic partners (opposite sex or same sex) that are willing to talk frankly about their long term relationship (of at least 20 years duration) and how it has evolved over time. The couple must be willing to have their answers audio-recorded. They must permit you to write about the interview. Although names and identifying information will be changed, the interview responses may be shared (with permission) with other students, incorporated in class materials, and analyzed for research that may ultimately be published. Your participants consent to be interviewed and to this use by reading and signing the consent form, which must be submitted by you.

After receiving permission, the student records an interview with the couple (together). Students ask a required set of questions (below) and use appropriate follow-up questions to gain information and insight. After reviewing the recording carefully, the student submits a written analysis and the audio recording. You are encouraged to share copies of the paper and the recording with the couple (if they want it).

Your job is to *really understand* the couple and their relationship. Try to have a "conversation," not just an interview. To the extent that the couple is comfortable answering them, ask follow up questions. You can and should ask *your own* questions (in addition to the required questions). What do *you* really want to know about long term relationships and how they change? However, be respectful of the couple's privacy. Do not pressure them to answer any question.

Important reminder. Students who cannot locate an appropriate couple, and those who prefer not to conduct an interview of this type, are <u>not</u> required to do so. Let the instructor know by the end of the first week of class. You will receive a different but equivalent assignment.

Instructions for Written Analysis

Submit a 4–6 (typed) **synthesis** of the interview responses and what you learned.

1. *Introduce:* Introduce the couple and describe their age of each partner, ethnicity of each partner, length of marriage and relationship, number of children, age of children, and indicate first or second marriage.
2. *Synthesize* responses within each section of the interview. Try not to simply repeat the questions and "regurgitate" the answers. Instead, within each section you should integrate the responses. Paraphrase. Interpret. Add your own observations. *Create a vivid portrait of the couple and how they described their relationship.* When they fit, use **class concepts to label and interpret** what the couple is telling you.

   Make sure you include **headings** for each section, such as "Background and Demographics," "Midlife Changes," "The Last Ten Years," "Advice to Younger Couples," and "Self Critique."

Include **detailed quotations** in each section to help convey the participants' points of view. However, most of the writing should be in **your
own** words.

3. *Analyze:* Use the frameworks (Relational Dialectics, Resilience, Role
Theory) from *Marriage at Midlife* to analyze the material you collected.
The theories might help you explain how the couple stayed together,
the challenges they have experienced over the years, or the ways the
relationships have changed (or not).

4. *Self-critique:* The last section of the paper should address the interview
procedure itself. How did you do as an interviewer? Did some questions
work better than others? Did the participants seem comfortable? Could
they answer the questions? What might you do differently next time to
gather more or better information? Use information from your research
methods classes to help you here.

References

Braun, V., & Clarke, V. (2006). Using thematic analysis in psychology. *Qualitative Research Psychology, 3*, 77–101.

Burgers, C. (2016). Conceptualizing change in communication through metaphor. *Journal of Communication, 66*, 250–265. doi:10.1111/jcom.12211

Glaser, B. G., & Strauss, A. L. (1967). *The discovery of grounded theory: Strategies for qualitative research.* New York, NY: Aldine Transaction.

Glucksberg, S., & McGlone, M. S. (1999). When love is not a journey: What metaphors mean. *Journal of Pragmatics, 31*(12), 1541–1558. doi:10.1016/S0378-2166(99)00003-X

Kelley, D. K. (2015). Chapter 4: Just relationships. In V. R. Waldron & D. K. Kelley (Eds.), *Moral talk across the lifespan: Creating good relationships* (pp. 75–94). New York, NY: Peter Lang.

Lakoff, G., & Johnson, M. (1980/2003). *Metaphors we live by.* Chicago, IL: The University of Chicago Press.

Lucas, K., & Buzzanell, P. M. (2012). Memorable messages of hard times: Constructing short- and long-term resiliences through family communication. *Journal of Family Communication, 12*, 189–208. doi:10.1080/15267431.2012.687196

Masten, A. S. (2001). Ordinary magic: Resilience processes in development. *American Psychologist, 56*, 227–238.

Smith, R. C., & Eisenberg, E. (1987). Conflict at Disneyland: A root metaphor analysis. *Communication Monographs, 54*, 367–380.

Steen, G. J., Dorst, A. G., Herrmann, J. B., Kaal, A. A., & Krennmayr, T. (2010). Metaphor in usage. *Cognitive Linguistic, 21*, 765–796. doi:10.1515/cogl.2010.024

Strauss, A., & Corbin, J. (1998). *Basics of qualitative research: Techniques and procedures for developing grounded theory* (2nd ed.). Thousand Oaks, CA: Sage.

INDEX

LIFESPAN
COMMUNICATION
Children, Families, and Aging

Thomas J. Socha, *General Editor*

From first words to final conversations, communication plays an integral and significant role in all aspects of human development and everyday living. The Lifespan Communication: Children, Families, and Aging series seeks to publish authored and edited scholarly volumes that focus on relational and group communication as they develop over the lifespan (infancy through later life). The series will include volumes on the communication development of children and adolescents, family communication, peer-group communication (among age cohorts), intergenerational communication, and later-life communication, as well as longitudinal studies of lifespan communication development, communication during lifespan transitions, and lifespan communication research methods. The series includes college textbooks as well as books for use in upper-level undergraduate and graduate courses.

Thomas J. Socha, Series Editor | *tsocha@odu.edu*
Kathryn Harrison, Acquisitions Editor | *kathryn.harrison@plang.com*

To order other books in this series, please contact our Customer Service Department at:

(800) 770-LANG (within the U.S.)
(212) 647-7706 (outside the U.S.)
(212) 647-7707 FAX

Or browse online by series at www.peterlang.com